# contents

# introduction

We didn't realize it when we started, but this has turned out to be a book with a message: New York has the most wide-ranging selection of desserts in the world to choose from. And if you're not actively seeking them out, you're missing one of the greatest—and most affordable—joys the city has to offer.

This is a far cry from stopping by the desserts section in your local grocery and throwing a few thousand calories into the cart. Or tagging dessert on as an afterthought when you've already overspent and overeaten.

One of the surprises to us has been that so many of Manhattan's most highly regarded restaurants welcome diners who come for dessert alone. They hope you won't come at the peak of the lunch or dinner rush, but why would you want to? They may seat you in the bar or lounge area; that's fine. The restaurateurs who've risen to the top are still concerned with their image and your satisfaction. For you, it's a way to test out a multistar restaurant at a price that doesn't require a second mortgage. An even thriftier option is searching out the city's scattered first-class bakeries, more and more of which are being opened under the aegis of established big-name restaurants.

So instead of flying to Paris for an authentic napoleon or taking the Orient Express to Vienna for Sacher torte, you're ready to 50+Best it. Here are a few tips that will help you get the most pleasure out of the experience.

❉ **Make it easy on yourself.** Some of these places are still well-kept secrets, some aren't. Plan a time when they're not likely to be mobbed. If you're going to one of the more heavily booked restaurants, call ahead and tell them you're coming for dessert. (All the restaurants in this book assured us they would accommodate dessert-only diners.) This is not so they can preordain you a seat in Siberia; it allows them to schedule their turnover accordingly (potentially an advantage for you).

❊ **Leave room for dessert.** That doesn't mean eating one drumstick less. A great dessert is worth building up an appetite for. Think of these uncommon desserts as something to have instead of, not in addition to, a large order of fries.

❊ **Relax.** Sure, you're better off having a fine pastry than a chemical compound if you're procrastinating or compensating for a bad hair day. But these desserts deserve better than that. Give them a time of their own.

❊ **Talk about it.** It is amazing how people perk up when you turn the subject to desserts. We've found you can engage even the chilliest conversationalist's attention just by asking, "What's your favorite place to go for dessert in New York?" In fact it's led us to most of the places in this book.

# the fabulous four

As it happens, New York's four most popular restaurants (as voted in New York's most popular restaurant guide) are uniformly happy to welcome dessert-seekers entering their imposing doors. All share a true passion for giving themselves and their patrons pleasure. All rely on the highest quality of fresh, seasonal ingredients, which they spend a lot of time, care, and money in assembling. It probably could go without saying that they all take pride in serving up the crème de la crème of desserts in New York.

## gramercy tavern

* *42 East 20th Street bet. Broadway and Park Avenue South*
PHONE: 212-477-0777
CREDIT CARDS: AmEx, DC, Disc, MC, V
PRICE: $8

Baked cannelloni with ricotta, pears, brown butter caramel sauce, and thyme ice cream. Fennel-raisin bread pudding drizzled with caramel sauce and crowned with Riesling-raisin crème fraiche. Warm rhubarb tart with basil syrup and rhubarb sorbet. Pastry chef Michelle Antonisek's heart is obviously with the land, and what she creates from its daily bounty is one of the wonders of New York's culinary landscape—desserts that are at once daring and comforting, homey and sophisticated. One particularly nice thing about the urban-country Tavern Room is that it doesn't discriminate between diners and desserters. No reservations are taken. Prepare to wait for your reward along with everyone else.

# union square café

❉ *21 East 16th Street bet. Union Square West and Fifth Avenue*

PHONE: 212-243-4020

CREDIT CARDS: AmEx, DC, Disc, MC, V

PRICE RANGE: $8.50; cookie plate, $7.50

Before restaurateur Danny Meyer created Gramercy Tavern he created Union Square Café. Its standards are as high as they ever were, and its patrons as loyal as the queen's corgis. The secret for avoiding the reservations telephone-line log-jam: Don't call ahead; they don't accept reservations for sitting at the bar anyway. All it takes is a bit of smart timing to claim an empty seat. Your only frustration is having to choose from among pastry chef Deborah Snyder's enticing, good-as-they-get daily delights. The malted chocolate pudding with Devil's Food cake? A pineapple upside-down cake plus a caramel pineapple fritter with cheesecake ice cream? Of course, you probably can't do better than USC's perennial banana tart with honey-vanilla ice cream and macadamia brittle. Then again, with the Union Square greenmarket just steps from the kitchen, you might never have the chance to get one of the day's more exotic combinations again. Ah, the problems life can bring.

# gotham bar & grill

❉ *12 East 12th Street bet. Fifth Avenue and Broadway*

PHONE: 212-620-4020

CREDIT CARDS: AmEx, DC, MC, V

PRICE RANGE: $10.50–11

Who said good things don't last? Almost two decades have passed since Alfred Portale first began piling plates high with his trail-blazing ventures into contemporary American cuisine. And he's still rousing the palates and passions of New York's gourmet cognoscenti, afternoons and evenings, at his landmark Gotham Bar & Grill. The room is a wide-open space, minimally and boldly conceived. The magic is in the attention to detail—like those ebonized maple trays that define your individual place at the bar. The same can be said for pastry chef Deborah Racicot's precisionist, lick-the-plate, flavorful desserts: her cannolis filled with cinnamon ricotta and pistachio ice cream, mellifluously blended with Meyer lemon gelée and blood orange sorbet. Her perfect tiramisu, served with warm chocolate madeleines and mocha granité. The once-and-for-always Gotham chocolate cake, made young again with a scoop of chicory ice cream. An especially nice destination after the theater, when the crowds have gone and the tables are open to all.

~~~~~~~~~~~~~~~~~~~~~~~~~~~~~~~~~~~~~~~~~~~~~~~~~~~

## daniel

❈ *60 East 65th Street bet. Madison and*
   *Park Avenues*
   PHONE: 212-288-0033
   CREDIT CARDS: AmEx, DC, MC, V
   PRICE RANGE: $12–14

"So beautiful!" That will be your reaction the first time you step through Daniel's famous doors. Housed and decorated in palatial neo-Renaissance style, Daniel is haute in every sense of the word, reaching its pinnacle, appropriately, in the flawlessly prepared, innovative French-inspired cuisine of celebrated chef-owner Daniel Boulud. It may seem incredible that you can indulge in one of pastry chef Eric Bertoia's ravishing desserts, in so sumptuous a setting, for—what? under $25 a person, including coffee and tip. Among recent arrivals on the constantly changing seasonal menu: banana-manjari chocolate clafoutis with macadamia nougat and caramel ice cream; mango and raspberry vacherin with ginger ice cream. The dark chocolate caramel bombe with passionfruit cream is the enduring classic. "So, where did you go last night?" "Daniel, and we had such a wonderful time." You bet!

These four restaurants deserve their continuing success and their exalted status in *New York's 50+ Best Places to Enjoy Dessert.*

# ❋new york's 50+ best

## *(A to Z)*

# amy's bread

❋ *672 Ninth Avenue bet. 46th and 47th Streets*
PHONE: 212-977-2670

❋ *972 Lexington Avenue bet. 70th and 71st Streets*
PHONE: 212-537-0270

CASH ONLY

*See also Chelsea Market*

PRICE RANGE: cake slices, bars, cookies, $2.25–4; whole
9-inch cakes, $35–40

Amy Scherber's bread is justly famous, but her homey all-American desserts deserve accolades as well. The best selections are available in her Hell's Kitchen and Upper East Side bakery cafes serving breakfast (scones, muffins, sticky buns, croissants) and lunch (fourteen sandwiches). For dessert (takeout, of course, if you wish) are six different kinds of layer cake, including old-fashioned yellow cake with chocolate icing, Devil's Food with chocolate silk icing, carrot cake with cream cheese frosting, coconut cake, and red-velvet cake filled with buttercream. There are lemon bars too, and butterscotch cashew bars, brownies, and great big cookies that you'd expect to come out of a home kitchen: Kitchen Sink, dark & white chocolate, oatmeal, and coconut pecan. Amy says she uses slightly less sugar than many bakers to allow the real flavor of ingredients—real butter and good chocolate—to come through. It does!

# angelica kitchen

※ *300 East 12th Street bet. First and Second Avenues*
PHONE: 212-228-2909
CASH ONLY
PRICE RANGE: $4–5

"Once a month, when the moon is full, a luscious chocolate dessert . . . appears on the menu at Angelica Kitchen." So reads the introduction to the recipe for chocolate layer cake with chocolate frosting in *The Angelica Home Kitchen Cookbook*. You can be sure that fans of this vegan restaurant keep track of lunar phases in order not to miss this specialty. Owner Leslie McEachern changes her dessert menu daily, but her loyal clientele doesn't seem to mind, whether it's pumpkin cheesecake (a mildly sweet and spicy wedge that we enjoyed on one visit), or tofu rhubarb cheesecake with strawberry sauce and hazelnut praline, or pistachio coconut tart, or any one of the great apple or spice cakes with maple tofu cream sauce and raspberry sauces. One of Angelica's most popular desserts is *kanten* parfait with nut cream, a gelled fruit dessert prepared using summer fruits or ripe pears. McEachern obtains as much of her produce as possible from local purveyors, not only organic farms in New York and Pennsylvania, but also sea vegetables from Maine, and maple syrup from northern Vermont. The glass-fronted restaurant is usually buzzing, and at dinner hour you can expect a wait for one of the rustic wooden tables. There's a large "family" table as well, for those seeking social interaction (although the management suggests that emotionally charged subjects should be avoided). No problem—think dessert.

# @sqc

❋ *270 Columbus Avenue bet. 72nd and 73rd Streets*
PHONE: 212-579-0100
CREDIT CARDS: AmEx, MC, V
PRICE RANGE: $7–9; $4 for the hot chocolate

The best-selling "dessert" at @SQC is their Famed Hot Chocolate—priced at just $4. Even the most hardened "I-don't-eat-dessert" stoics find that hard to resist. In fact, everything about @SQC is pretty irresistible. Admittedly, the enclosed sidewalk sunroom exterior and unadorned dining room don't look that different from their cafe neighbors. The locals who stop by to nosh resemble the West Side neighborhood crowd. Except they often include neighbors like Keanu, Jerry, and Naomi.

The attraction? No pretense. A passion to please. Fair prices. And imaginative riffs on the beloved staples of traditional American cooking. For desserts, @SQC's A-list of ingredients—from their secret sourcebook of artisanal purveyors—includes seasonal berries, caramel, maple, toasted walnuts, and chocolate.

Always on the menu is the doubly indulgent chocolate gateau with hot chocolate ice cream. Apple crisp pie is pure American nostalgia in perfect harmony: a high-standing individual apple pie, its crust flaky-crumbly, plus caramel ice cream, caramel sauce—and a wedge of limited-edition Vermont cheddar cheese. A walnut tart comes with Vermont maple ice cream. Robichon cheese is an astonishing addition to the blackberry tart.

The seasonal list goes on. But the seating doesn't. @SQC is cozy, with a long bar to the left. Chances are that affable owner-host Linda Campbell will stop by to chat. And owner-chef Scott Campbell will wander through to make sure everyone is happy. Incidentally, the more recognizable celebrities tend to dine in the afternoon and late-evening hours. Follow their lead.

# balthazar

※ *Spring Street bet. Broadway and Crosby Streets*
PHONE: 212-965-1414
CREDIT CARDS: AmEx, MC, V
PRICE RANGE: lunch desserts, $5.50–7.50

It was snowing outside the Spring Street windows the last time we stopped in at Balthazar—with no reservation—on a late winter afternoon. As we sank our forks through the yielding layers of caramelized bananas over a silken risotto cream on a crunchy butter crust, New York seemed roughly two thousand miles away.

Huge age-speckled mirrors on the walls. Long red-leather banquettes along the walls. Serpentine-topped glass-and-wood partitions to create intimate spaces. Terrazzo tiling underfoot and slowly revolving circular fans overhead. Every detail works in this wildly popular homage to the great fin-de-siècle Parisian brasseries.

The desserts are exactly what you want them to be: richly taste-and-textured recreations of the long-time staples of French bistro fare—a lightly brittle veneer atop an unctuous crème brûlée; an airy pavlova, its wispy meringue piled high with seasonal berries; profiteroles in a pool of good chocolate sauce; the freshest of buttery berry tarts.

Balthazar opens its doors at 7:30 a.m. and closes them after midnight on most days. Unless you love mobs and waits, pick an hour when *tout le monde* is unlikely to decide to join you there, and call ahead. It is an addictive experience.

## balthazar boulangerie

❋ *80 Spring Street bet. Broadway and Crosby Street*

PHONE: 212-965-1785

CREDIT CARDS: AmEx, MC, V

PRICE RANGE: slices of cake, $5; small tart, $5; large tart, $20

The turn-of-the-century décor and spirit of Balthazar spill over into the bakery, just next door. Its showcases and display stands overflow with take-away treasures, facing a customer area that makes a rush-hour elevator seem like a wide open space. The struggle is worth it. All the Francophile temptations are there, and over to the left a blackboard announces the ever-changing seasonal specials. When we last looked, a lattice galette with orange marmalade-glazed pink rhubarb and bright red strawberries on puff pastry celebrated spring, along with Easter surprises like chocolate and hazelnut praline stuffed into genuine egg shells ($84 a dozen).

## black hound

❋ *170 Second Avenue at 11th Street*

PHONE: 212-979-9505

CREDIT CARDS: AmEx, MC, V

PRICE RANGE: pastries, $7; large pies and tarts, under $28; and chocolate truffles, $8.75 per quarter pound

This elegant patisserie is a fairly recent addition to the East Village's eclectic and ever more gentrified mix. Under a discreet black awning, the window fairly pulsates with forbidden pleasures—chocolate cakes, nut cakes, cheese cakes, fruit pies, cream pies, fruit tarts, nut tarts, rum balls, mud balls, snowballs, cookies, candies and confections. What's best? The Busy Bee chocolate cake is most popular (chocolate mousse, almond cake, marzipan, and almond liqueur), but we vote for the stunningly beautiful chocolate berry cup, a jumbo tea cup made of chocolate and filled with almond cake, raspberry sauce, lemon curd, and whipped cream and bejeweled with glistening fresh fruits. Irresistible as a special dessert to share with a friend or to bring as a gift when a knockout gift is called for. Given the complexity of many of Black Hound's desserts, they are surprisingly affordable.

# blue hill

�֎ *75 Washington Place bet. MacDougal Street and Sixth Avenue*
PHONE: 212-539-1776
CREDIT CARDS: AmEx, DC, MC, V
PRICE: $25

The attractive and intimate Blue Hill, just off Washington Square, has had a brilliant idea, and one long overdue in the restaurant business, we might add. Every evening after 9:30, they shine a spotlight on a special dessert offering, inviting you to come in for a $25 multicourse extravaganza of beautifully presented sweets prepared by pastry chef Pierre Reboul. Although the individual components may vary, you can expect the first course to be a palate-cleansing sorbet. On our visit it was an elegant lychee-champagne sorbet with a sauce of Riesling jelly and one crystallized rose petal to nibble on as a floral accent to the sweet wine flavors. Next came a tray of three plates, each holding a different mini dessert to be eaten left to right to ensure the correct progression of flavors. We took the suggestion, starting with a surprising tri-layered torte: a base of crushed avocado supports tart lime sorbet and lime syrup topped with a thin crust of salty caramel. Center stage was a round of chocolate brioche bread pudding with a dollop of vanilla ice cream; and at far right, fruit rolls, strawberry and mango flavored, filled with strawberry sorbet and mango-cardamom sorbet. Next up, rhubarb soup in an espresso cup made with red wine and port infused with lemon grass and mint and topped with a melting mini scoop of cheese sorbet—equal parts fromage blanc, crème fraiche, and mascarpone. Finally, (yes, finally), came a hot-from-the-oven passionfruit soufflé about the size of a small cupcake, but oh, so much better. Did we say "finally"? There's just one more lovely thing: a plate of tiny, just-baked warm financiers nestled in a folded white linen napkin and accompanied by a pot of fresh rhubarb preserves, which we ate with eyes wide shut.

## After the Theater

"We don't go out for dessert after the theater," a grumpy know-it-all informed us. "They won't give you just dessert."

Is he ever wrong! And what a pleasure he's depriving himself of!

Concerning the "wrong" part: Even the chicest, most heavily booked restaurants are likely to welcome you with open arms after 10:30 or so, in this increasingly early-to-bed city. Chelsea's small and thriving Red Cat, for one, couldn't quite promise they'd give up seats for dessert-only at the prime-time dinner hours. But later? Sure, especially during the week.

Again, our best advice is to call ahead and ask, if you can. If you can't, just show up and smile. It's worked for us every time.

Obviously it's a pleasure, whether you're prolonging the high of a great evening of theater or compensating for a bummer. The bonus: By the time you finish dessert, it'll be easier to get a cab.

# blue smoke

❋ *116 East 27th Street between Park Avenue South and Lexington Avenue*
PHONE: 212-447-7733
CREDIT CARDS: AmEx, MC, V
PRICE RANGE: $7–8

When it comes to desserts, expectations don't run high at Manhattan's BBQ joints—unless Danny Meyer, owner of the Gramercy Tavern and Union Square Café, is at the helm. Down-home doesn't get any better 'round these parts than at his "urban barbecue," Blue Smoke.

That doesn't mean that pastry chef Jennifer Giblin hasn't tempered things to suit New Yorkers' refined sensibilities. Could they be serving sticky toffee pudding drenched in roasted pecans, Blue Smoke's signature dessert, with a big dollop of crème fraiche in Amarillo roadhouses?

Are they flying in artisanal chocolate to mix with the Valrhona cocoa powder for the blowtorch-glazed frosting on a chocolate layer cake? (Ma'am, that is good!) Maybe green-tomato pie, with the lightest of lard-and-butter crusts, is close to some original. We're not going to Texas to find out.

The atmosphere here is just-right casual, with no wagon wheels in sight. Ties are tolerated. Flying beer bottles are not.

## jazz standard

❊ *116 East 27th Street*

PHONE: 212-576-2232

If you prefer your desserts accompanied by some of the best jazz in New York, you'll find it downstairs from Blue Smoke at Jazz Standard, with sets beginning at 7:30 each evening. Same dessert menu. Cover charge, but no minimum.

# bread bar

❊ *11 Madison Avenue at 25th Street*

PHONE: 212-889-0667

CREDIT CARDS: AmEx, MC, V

PRICE RANGE: Bread Bar, $6–8; Tabla, $8–9

A leisurely stroll through the area around Lexington Avenue and 27th and 28th Streets should turn up a pretty fair sampling of Indian pastries and sweets as they are served all over New York. Even a stop at Kalustyan, one of the city's most popular and well-stocked Indian groceries/delis/bakeries, is itself a culinary cultural education.

Leave it to Danny Meyer to take some of the basics—the spices, seeds, fruits, and flavors of India—and turn them into the unique cross-cultural cuisine at Bread Bar. We chose Bread over the more elegant Tabla upstairs because pastry chef Susan Davis's desserts there stay a bit closer to their Indian roots, it's less formal, and it's more fun. Drop in any time after noon and you'll find Tahitian vanilla bean kulfi, an unctuously thick vanilla ice cream, in a glistening pomegranate syrup spotted with sour cherries. Even richer (if that's possible) is the dulce de leche "kulfi pop," coated in dark chocolate and resting in a pool of caramel sauce. It makes the warm, featherweight doughnut holes, served with seasonal fruit compote, seem positively dietetic.

The room is a jumble of muted colors, natural materials, and eclectic styles, all very unintimidating.

## tamarind café

❉ *43 East 22nd Street bet. Broadway and Park Avenue South*
PHONE: 212-674-7400
CREDIT CARDS: AmEx, MC, V
PRICE RANGE: $5

This modest appendage to the highly admired, upscale Indian restaurant Tamarind is the real thing, with a small selection of traditional Indian pastries, here made with a lighter, surer hand than New Yorkers are accustomed to. Each is accompanied on the menu by a recommended selection from the extensive tea offerings. Among the cafe desserts is *paysam*, a saffron-flavored vermicelli pudding with caramelized almonds. Creamlike in texture, it is rich-rich-rich. On request, you can also order dessert from the regular restaurant menu. We sampled the *ghujjia*, a light pastry stuffed with a lovely blend of semolina, raisins, coconut, and cashew nuts, with lemon sauce. The atmosphere is sleekly modern, with a few contemporary Indian prints for a cool touch of the East and huge mirrors and windows to give the small space an expansive atmosphere.

# bruno bakery

❋ *506 LaGuardia Place bet. Bleecker and Houston Streets*
PHONE: 212-982-5854

# pasticceria bruno

❋ *245 Bleecker Street bet. Leroy and Carmine Streets*
PHONE: 212-242-4959
www.brunobaker.com
CREDIT CARDS: AmEx, MC, V
PRICE RANGE: pastries, $2–$3.50; minis, $1.25; whole cakes, $20–137 (whole sheet cakes)

Award-winning Biagio Settepani took over at Bruno Bakery cafe and pasticceria in 1981, and has been turning out Italian pastry of consistently high quality ever since: freshly filled cannoli oozing with ricotta cream studded with chocolate chips and citron; *sfogliatelle* (crunchy clam-shaped layered pastries filled with ricotta and farina—best eaten warm); *zuppetta* (puff pastry layers filled with rum-flavored custard); and the so-called lobster tails, humongous crustacean-shaped shells filled with hazelnut cream. Chef Settepani provides French specialties as well, such as fruit tarts, chocolate mousse, crème brûlée, and mille-feuille; and with a nod to the Latin dessert trend, dulce de leche cheesecake with a milky caramel flavor. There are cookies, biscotti, sorbets, and gelatos, too.

Desserts at the bakery and pasticceria are much the same, but items at the latter location sometimes yield fancier flourishes. The cannoli for example, in classic Sicilian style, are dipped in pistachio nuts on one end and candied orange peel on the other. With or without the trimmings, Chef Settepani's cannoli are so darned good we wondered why. Is it simply the rich, mildly tangy filling or is it the fact that the shell is correctly made with Marsala wine? We're not the only ones to recognize his talents.

> In 2000, Chef Settepani was named one of the best pastry chefs in America by *Pastry Art & Design* and *Chocolatier* magazines. He teaches classes in Biscotti and Panettone at the New School, should you wish to learn dolci arts from a master.

## The Dolci Circuit

In the search for New York's best dolci, two East Village institutions, DeRobertis and Veniero's—just a cannoli's throw from each other—demand attention and respect. The product is comparable but the ambience differs mightily. **DeRobertis** (176 First Ave. at 11th St., 212-674-7137), founded in 1904 and still looking rather turn-of-the-twentieth-century, is a quiet tile-floored bakery with cafe tables in back that attract neighborhood people looking for a peaceful place to read the paper while enjoying espresso or cappuccino and, say, a piece of very good ricotta cheesecake or a *sfogliatella*. **Veniero's Pasticceria and Caffe** (342 East 11th St. bet. First and Second Aves., 212-674-7070), established as a bakery around the same time, is more of a scene, with take-a-number lines at the front counter and cafe-goers filling the back area with lively conversation. The East Side Italian grocery store **Agata & Valentina** (1505 First Ave. at 79th St., 212-452-0690) sells moist ricotta cheesecake by the pound at their small espresso cafe, as well as other types of dolci worth exploring (shop during the week if possible to avoid the weekend crush and snaking checkout lines). Well worth a trip out to Brooklyn's Little Italy in Bensonhurst is Sicilian-owned **Villabate Pasticceria & Bakery** (7117 18th Ave. bet. 71st and 72nd Sts.; 718-331-8430), which has gained the kudos of numerous New York baking kingpins and chefs who say the authentic confections are incomparable. At nearby **Alba Italian Pastry Shoppe** (7001 18th Ave. at 70th St.; 718-232-2122), a free cup of coffee gives you time to sip and ponder the choices: excellent cannoli, and much more. In the Bronx, **Egidio Pastry Shop** (622 East 187th St.; 718-295-6077) in the Arthur Avenue area is renowned for, you guessed it, cannoli!

## café des artistes

❋ *1 West 67th Street bet. Columbus Avenue and Central Park West*
PHONE: 212-877-3500
CREDIT CARDS: AmEx, MC, V
PRICE RANGE: $10–14

Café des Artistes doesn't recreate a lost era in restaurant history. It's the real thing.

Howard Chandler Christy's famous murals of lightly clad nymphs cavorting in flowery bowers were not started until 1934. But the artist had been one of the Hotel des Artistes' colorful tenants when the restaurant opened in 1917. Since then, the restaurant has welcomed everyone from Marcel Duchamp and Isadora Duncan to today's great stars of the nearby Metropolitan Opera—and now you, if you're feeling fin-de-siècle (and flush). The chocolate napoleon, an extravagance of ice cream freshly sandwiched between two oversize flaky pastry triangles, sits in a sea of chocolate sauce sprinkled with fresh berries. A trio of crème brûlées—classic, lavender, and chocolate—is lighter and, at $10, thriftier.

If you're preparing your children for the high life, bring them for Café des Artistes' renowned hot fudge sundae. For the young and playful, this is a "construct-it-yourself" dream, with the ice cream, fudge, nuts, and whipped cream served in separate bowls. It's not on the menu. You have to ask.

There is a small parlor bar off to one side of the lobby. But the place you want to be is the multilevel main restaurant, with its gaslight fixtures, deep colors, conservatory plants, and murals. Pick an off-peak hour and tell them you're coming. They'll understand.

## steak house at monkey bar

✳ *60 East 54th Street bet. Madison and Park Avenues*
PHONE: 212-838-2600
CREDIT CARDS: AmEx, MC, V
PRICE RANGE: $7.50–10.50

Café des Artistes isn't the only place you can go for a taste of the dessert high life as it was lived in New York's gilded past. Over at the Monkey Bar, the colorful creatures that gave this legendary watering spot its name in the 1930s are still frolicking across the walls. Now, where Tallulah Bankhead, Joe DiMaggio, and Marlon Brando once sipped a martini or threw back a scotch, you can indulge in some of the most magnificent desserts of the last century: a skyline-peaked Baked Alaska surrounded by delicate spun sugar sculptures; a perfect flower of caramelized banana petals outlining the Floating Island in a sea of spiced rum sauce; a basket of key lime cream pie with a perfect poppyseed cookie handle, so exquisitely crafted you can hardly bear cutting into it. Pastry Chef Thomas Paulino is recreating a lost art from the Age of Elegance. And, yes, they are delicious.

# palm court at the plaza
❋ *768 Fifth Avenue at 59th Street*
PHONE: 212-759-3000
CREDIT CARDS: AmEx, MC, V
PRICE RANGE: $9.75

At least once in your life, you must experience New York's Gilded Age as it survives in the Plaza Hotel's opulent Palm Court. Sitting in its upholstered armchairs amid the soaring marble columns and palm trees, thick carpeting under your feet and a uniformed waiter hovering at your side, for an hour or two you imagine what life at the top must once have been like. You can make your selection from a table groaning under its platters of mousses, tortes, and tatins. Such luxury comes at a price. Pay it. Remember, here money is no object.

# café lalo
❋ *201 West 83rd Street bet. Amsterdam Avenue and Broadway*
PHONE: 212-496-6031
www.cafelalo.com
CASH ONLY
PRICE RANGE BY THE SLICE: cakes, $4.95; tarts, $5.50; pies, $4.95; cheesecakes, $4.95; bundt and coffee cakes, $4.25; ice cream or frozen yogurt per scoop, $1.95

West Siders have known of this dessert trove for years; for neighborhood newcomers, it's a revelation: more than one hundred kinds of cakes, pies, and tarts, including twenty-seven varieties of cheesecake. Then there are the cookies, pastries, rugelach, cannoli, biscotti, brownies, ice creams, zabaglione, frozen yogurt, fresh berries, and milkshakes! Cappuccino and espresso? Of course!

Styled as a Parisian cafe with floor-to-ceiling windows, it's so pretty that it's often selected as a location for commercials and movies, most notably *Sleepless in Seattle* with Tom Hanks and Meg Ryan.

Brunch is served daily from 9 a.m. to 4 p.m., and the newly expanded bar provides its evening crowd with a large selection of dessert wines, aperitifs, and other types of after-dinner drinks.

With so much to offer, Café Lalo tends to attract people in large numbers, including moms with strollers, and the service can be slow and a bit snippy. But you're here for dessert, and that's where your focus should be. Chocolate figures prominently in the offerings, with mousse cakes flavored with everything from Bailey's Irish Cream to passionfruit. The Viennese raspberry mousse cake is outstanding.

# café sabarsky

❖ *1048 Fifth Avenue at 86th Street*
PHONE: 212-628-6200
CREDIT CARDS: AmEx, MC, V
PRICE RANGE: $5–7

In just over two years, Café Sabarsky has established itself as such a fixture on the New York scene that it's hard to imagine a time when it wasn't here. Part of that comes from its setting, within the high-paneled library of the stately Miller-Vanderbilt mansion overlooking Central Park.

More important is the minute attention that chef-owner Kurt Gutenbrunner has devoted to every detail in recreating the ambience and cuisine of its old-world Viennese counterparts. It shows in the precisely reproduced Wiener Werkstätte fixtures, the crisp white napery, the chairs, and china, all Austrian-made.

Finally, it all comes down to the food. And the desserts, each a classic, are as authentic and delicious as anything you'll find within Vienna's Ringstrasse: Sacher torte, the moist dark, chocolate-robed cake with apricot confiture, just as it originated at Vienna's Hotel Sacher. Apfelstrudel, the cafe's best-seller, its pastry cocoon as tender as the succulent apples within. Topfontorte, a cheesecake that actually tastes of the farmer's cheese with which it's made, garnished with fresh poached pear. Everything, naturally, *mit schlag*, freshly whipped.

Klimttorte, the ultra-rich medley of chocolate butter cream and hazelnut ganache, serves as a reminder that Café Sabarsky shares both the quarters and cultural heritage of the Neue Gallerie, the handsome museum founded by Serge Sabarsky and Ronald Lauder devoted to the vibrant art of early twentieth-century Germany and Austria.

A hint: Café Sabarsky doesn't take reservations for lunch, and you may face a wait. Go a little later, and consider ordering two desserts; at a bargain $6-ish each, you can indulge yourself.

## wallsé

✴ *West 11th Street at Washington Street*
PHONE: 212-352-2300
CREDIT CARDS: AmEx, MC, V
PRICE RANGE: $8

Kurt Gutenbruner has a second outpost of his Austro-Hungarian culinary empire on a quiet corner in the far West Village. At Wallsé, open for dinner only, the emphasis is less on the classic Kaffeehaus desserts. Apfelstrudel is a menu constant, as is the luscious Salzburger Nokerl, featherweight sweet dumplings showered with raspberry sauce. If Mohr im Hemd is on the menu, that's the chocoholic's dessert of choice, a chocolate hazelnut soufflé-like cake served warm from the oven.

## carrot top

※ *3931 Broadway bet. 164th and 165th Streets*
PHONE: 212-927-4800

※ *5025 Broadway bet. 213th and 214th Streets
(the original twenty-three-year-old location)*
PHONE: 212-569-1532
CREDIT CARDS: AmEx, Disc, MC, V
PRICE RANGE: cookies and cake slices, $1.95–2.95

*ATTENTION: All Customers Illegally Parked.
Please give us your orders, we will bring it to your car.
Traffic officers will give you a ticket!!*

So reads the sign over the counter of this longtime and well-loved bakery cafe in Washington Heights. It's the kind of place where everybody knows your name—or greets and treats you as though they did.

The name is the giveaway to what Carrot Top does best: carrot cake, speckled with nuts and spices, moist, scrumptious, and available whichever way you like it: a square slab, two layers, three layers, or "special," each slathered with old-fashioned whipped cream cheese frosting. There's even a carrot cookie, CD-sized (which is, basically, spread-out carrot cake). We broke open a carrot muffin late one morning right from the oven, a steamy cloud rising from its center.

There are all kinds of pies (including sweet potato, cherry crumb, and at holiday time, pecan) and cakes (Black Forest is now the best-seller), all made from recipes passed down from owner Renée Mancino's grandmother, and now on to Renée's daughter, Nikki.

Do your sampling in the functional main room or the slightly fancier green room off to the side. Or place your order and run for the car.

It's all the same at Carrot Top's original, twenty-three-year-old location.

## ceci-cela patisserie

❉ *55 Spring Street bet. Lafayette and Mulberry Streets*
PHONE: 212-274-9179
CREDIT CARDS: MC, V

❉ *166 Chambers Street bet. Broadway and Greenwich Street*
PHONE: 212-566-8933
CREDIT CARDS: AmEx, MC, V
PRICE RANGE: pastries, $2–5.75; cakes, individual, $3–5.75; mini pastries, $1.25

Opened in 1992, Ceci-Cela is the kind of place that seems to have been there forever and makes you wish you lived upstairs and could easily pop down for a perfect pain au chocolat every morning, and a piece of quiche at lunchtime (there's a tiny exposed-brick back room with a few tables) and any one of their truly wonderful pastries or cakes for dessert every night. The large talents behind the little space (two people can barely pass each other between the wall and the pastry case) are French chefs Laurent Dupal and Hervé Grall, both veterans of legendary restaurants owned by Drew Nieporent.

Best-sellers, and justly so, are the raspberry-and-blueberry tart and the light and lovely raspberry chocolate mousse cake; but the selections will test your resistance to such Gallic delicacies as the napoleon with fresh raspberries, and the crème brûlée with bergamot flavor. Dupal and Grall and Chef Gerard Fioravanti welcome special orders for personalized cakes; and when you're wondering what enchanting gift to bring to an exacting foodie friend, look no further than Ceci-Cela's Fancy Petit Fours Box of a dozen exquisite miniatures for $25.

# cendrillon

✳ *45 Mercer Street bet. Broome and Grand Streets*
PHONE: 212-343-9012
CREDIT CARDS: AmEx, Disc, MC, V
PRICE RANGE: $6.50-8

Once upon a time, SoHo was *the* place to go for the fresh, the unexpected, the stimulating, the exciting. At Cendrillon, it still is.

Here, behind a modest facade on the southernmost reaches of Mercer Street, one of New York's most adventuresome chefs continues to blur the lines between Eastern and Western cuisines. He's Romy Dorotan, and he brings the principles and techniques of the French cooking in which he was trained to the cuisine of his native Philippines. His success comes not only from his talent, but from his zeal in introducing an A-list of Philippine ingredients virtually unknown in the

United States. Cassava Bibingka with mangosteen-palm sugar ice cream is not something you improvise from the Union Square greenmarket.

What should you try? We loved the mango tart, Romy's version of the traditional tarte tatin—its paper-thin, crunchy, torched crust resting on top of a distinctively spiced sweet mango base. Buko pie—buko being young, unripened coconut—came with a fruity, barely sweet rhubarb sauce when we had it (accompanied by the chef's own vanilla bean ice cream). Buko sorbet accompanies a blueberry-and-ube (purple yam) tart. Kalamansi meringue pie is made from a mild variety of lime Romy brings in from the Philippines. For the most authentic experience—particularly on a hot summer day—dip into the Halo Halo, a kind of ice sundae, with coconut sport (a variety of very soft coconut flesh), agar-agar, jackfruit, sweet red beans, cocoa gel, palm seed, and toasted rice topped with ube ice cream.

Everyone from Alice Waters to Jean-Georges Von-gerichten has dropped by Cendrillon's low-key, sophisticated space to sample the exotic and modestly priced dinner menu. Dessert is the perfect start.

# chelsea market

Off the "main street" of this cavernous, seemingly hacked-out-of-rock, city-block-deep market you can find your cookies, your brownies, your cakes, pies, and fancy fruit tarts, and, oh yes, your ice cream, too. It's all made on premises. **Goupil & DeCarlo Patisserie** (212-807-1908) is a source of every imaginable type of fruit tart, small and large, plus mousse cakes, napoleons, and eclairs. PRICE RANGE: pastries and small tarts, $2.75–4; large tarts, $19–24. **Eleni's Cookies** (212-255-7990; www.elenis.com) is known for beautifully decorated hand-iced cookies (her fanciful designs or yours), homey, soft-baked sugar cookies (including snickerdoodles, chocolate chip, and oatmeal raisin), and heart-shaped "love" brownies. Also available at Dean & DeLuca, Grace's Marketplace, Bergdorf Goodman, Neiman Marcus, and Citarella. PRICE RANGE: regular cookies, $.60–1.25; designer cookies, $1.00 each. **Fat Witch Bakery** (212-807-1335, www.fatwitch.com): We taste-tested all eight varieties of Patricia Helding's cutely packaged, baked-on-premises brownies and our favorites were (drumroll, please) the basic no-nut brownie, fudgy and perfect; Red Witch, chock-full of luscious dried cherries; Walnut, the basic model plus crunch; and Java, chocolate with a coffee jolt. The shop also sells Brownie Babies, gift boxes and ships almost anywhere. PRICE RANGE: $1.25–2.50. **Sarabeth's Bakery** (212-989-2424, www.sarabeth.com): Here you'll find a sampling of the baked goods served at the other Sarabeth locations (see Index): sour cream, buttermilk, and cream cheese cakes, Bundt cakes, loaf cakes, cookies, and cupcakes. Chocolate favorites include a light chocolate soufflé cake and a rich and famous chocolate truffle cake. PRICE RANGE PER SLICE: about $4. **Amy's Bread** (212-977-2670, www.amys-bread.com): We often eat Amy Scherber's Semolina with Golden Raisins and Fennel Bread for dessert, it's that delicious; and you can get it, and all of her other extraordinarily good breads and some pastries at Chelsea Market—where her main bread-baking operation is located—but for a complete selection of her homey, American-style desserts you need to go to her other two locations (see page 12). **Ruthy's Bakery & Café** (212-463-8800): We like the rugelach (eight flavors), especially apricot and raspberry; the old-fashioned carrot cake is fine, as is the New York-style cheesecake; and if you're in a jam looking for a ready-made special-occasion cake, Ruthy's stocks a locker full, all on display at the back of the store. She also does special order cakes of any shape or design, from Pooh to a graduate's mortar board. PRICE RANGE: cookies and rugelach, $11.95/lb; cakes per slice, $2.95; whole cakes, $12.95-34.95. **Ronnybrook Dairy and Ice Cream** (212-741-6455, www.ronnybrook.com): Ronnybrook sells deliciously rich and always fresh organic ice creams using their "own cream from our cows," guaranteed free of any kind of bovine growth hormone. Cones are $1.35 (kids), $2.25 (single), $3.25 (double), and $3.50 (pints). Unusual flavors include cinnamon, cardamom ginger crème brûlée, and pumpkin.

# chez moha

✳ *230 Thompson Street bet. Bleecker and West Third Streets*
PHONE: 212-477-6562
CASH ONLY
PRICE RANGE: sorbets and ice creams, \$3.95–7.95
(sampler plate); cookies, \$3.95 (plate), \$16–18 (pound);
French pastries, \$3.95 each

Some of New York's most delicious and exotic sorbets are to be found, surprisingly, in this little Thompson Street "casbah," prepared by the hand of chef Moha Orchid (pronounced "mwah or-SHEED"), who, if you give him half a second, will proclaim his proud Moroccan Berber ancestry and recount his culinary resumé from Europe to New York, where in 1999 he opened Cookies and Couscous, now Chez Moha. Here, in a bright yellow room with red banquettes, he serves the dishes of his native Morocco—soups, tajines, and excellent couscous—along with a few pastries he makes on premises, and those not-to-be-missed sorbets.

No one who loves sorbet should fail to try chef Orchid's sampler plate that might include flavors like coconut amaretto toasted almond, lychee jalapeno raisin, pear orange poppyseed, and red plum anise. So fresh and packed with flavoring ingredients (Moroccan herbs and spices sent by the chef's mother), the sorbets fairly crumble on the plate. Unusual ice cream flavors include green tea fresh mint and vanilla toasted walnut.

# ciao bella café

❈ *27 East 92nd Street bet. Fifth and Madison Avenues*
PHONE: 212-831-5555

❈ *200 West 57th Street at Seventh Avenue*
PHONE: 212-956-5555

❈ *227 Sullivan Street bet. Bleecker and West 3rd Streets*
PHONE: 212-505-7100

❈ *81 Washington Street, Brooklyn*
PHONE: 718-222-9880

❈ *285 Mott Street*
PHONE: 212-505-7100
CASH ONLY
PRICE RANGE: small cup, $3.50; large cup, $4.25; pre-packed pint, $4.75

Ciao Bella may have gone national since its launch in SoHo in 1983, but it's still a small company (about eighty to one hundred employees nationwide) committed to small-batch gelato preparation. The headquarters are now located in New Jersey, where chef Danilo Zecchin of Torino, Italy, is in charge of both quality control and development of exciting new flavors, from espresso (made with Arabic coffee) to blackberry cabernet sorbet. The gelato remains a silky milk/cream-based product that contains 20 percent air as compared to 60 percent in most American brands, and contains only 12 percent butterfat versus 16 percent in typical ice cream. The sorbet is 70–80 percent fruit (in contrast to about 40 percent in American sorbets).

Among the dozens of unusual and exotic ice cream flavors you'll find at any one of the gelaterias are chocolate jalapeno, triple espresso, fromage blanc, and bourbon butter pecan. Among the sorbets, blood orange (made from Italian fruit), red grape, and chunky cherry are outstanding. The cherry, by the way, is made from Morello cherry puree with crunchy, juicy halves of Bordeaux black cherries nestled within. New sorbet flavors include rose-petal-and-lavender and kalamansi, made from a heavenly mild lime of that name that is native to the Philippines (see also the listing for Cendrillon).

Ciao Bella is the house brand at Sarabeth restaurants and is packaged and sold by the pint in upscale supermarkets.

## Ice cream? Gelato? What's the dif'?

Ice cream—such a simple pleasure, so easy to understand: take some cream, sweeten it up, freeze it and voila!—food of the gods. Then along came gelato—we loved it even while wondering what it was; and sorbet—isn't that sherbet? And what about good old frozen custard? Yes, ice cream has become complicated, but not hard to understand, and only more delicious in all its varieties with each passing day. Here's how the subject of quiescent desserts breaks down, with thanks to *Food Lover's Companion* by Sharon Tyler Herbst.

**Ice Cream:** The dairy product we know and love is made from cream and other milk products, such as condensed and dry milk. To this is added sugar or other sweeteners—in some cases honey or corn syrup or artificial sweeteners. Finally, solids are tossed in— chocolate chunks, nuts, fruit, and so forth. The FDA stipulates that ice creams with "solid additions" have at least 8 percent milk fat; 10 percent for plain ice creams. Ice cream also necessarily contains air—termed "overrun" by the FDA—to give it a soft, scoopable texture. Commercial ice creams may have overrun of between

20 to 50 percent, and may include emulsifiers, stabilizers, and artificial flavors, among other additions. The homemade ice creams served in many fine restaurants are free of additives.

**Ice Milk:** Basically ice cream with less milk fat and milk solids.

**Gelato:** Italian ice cream (the word literally means "iced" in Italian). Gelato contains less air and therefore has a denser, creamier texture than American ice cream. Egg yolk is sometimes used in gelato, but most often it's a milk/cream-based product.

**Gelateria:** A shop or cafe where gelato is sold.

**Sorbet:** The French word for a frozen, water-based confection that never contains milk and is usually made with fruit and fruit juices or other flavorings. The Italians call it *sorbetto*, which comes from the verb *sorbire*, meaning to "slush it up," appropriate to its lovely texture.

**Sherbet:** The same as sorbet, but a variation may contain milk, egg whites, and/or gelatin. The word is derived from the Arabic *sharbet* or *charbet*, a cold drink of sweetened fruit juice. The Arabs are said to have learned about cold or frozen desserts from the Chinese, who first thought of adding sweet flavorings to snow.

**French Ice Cream:** Ice cream with a base of egg custard.

**Frozen Custard:** Genuine frozen custard differs from ice cream in that it contains at least 1.4 percent egg yolk. Like ice cream it contains at least 10 percent milk fat, although many custards today are low-fat. The best frozen custard is made in a "continuous flow" machine that does not beat air into the mixture (see "Custard Beach" in entry for Grand Central Market).

**Granité, Granita:** see Ice.

**Ice:** An ice (as in lemon ice), is a water-based frozen confection with a relatively low sugar content and a more granular texture than sorbet.

# citarella the restaurant

❖ *1240 Sixth Avenue at 49th Street*
PHONE: 212-332-1515
CREDIT CARDS: AmEx, MC, V
PRICE RANGE: main desserts, $9–15; Asian desserts, $8

Pastry chef Bill Yosses believes that the last course of a meal needs to be the most enticing: "Dessert adds another dimension just at the point when conversation and group dynamics heat up." The problem is, when his delectable, deconstructed plated desserts arrive at the table, the conversation tends to collapse into "umms" and "wows." Even if you order the toasted lemon pound cake with fresh raspberry sauce and lemon ice cream or the chocolate brioche pudding with maple ice cream and chocolate sauce, or the pineapple-banana upside-down pecan cake with coconut sorbet—all of which have become signature creations—you may first receive a palate-cleansing pre-dessert sorbet "to get you into the dessert state of mind." It might arrive as a fruity blood orange-elderflower-muscat grape-champagne smoothie in a long-stemmed crystal flute. You want to make this last as long as possible, but then the main dessert arrives, arranged in parts like a small town awaiting excavation with a silver spoon. The concluding plate of petit fours seems an anticlimax, except for a thimble full of crimson liquid—hibiscus tisane with a layer of lychee foam the color of smoke, a typical touch of Yosses's exoticism.

Citarella's elegant vanilla-colored second-floor dining room—decorated with charming "portholes" that hold blue-water shell still lifes—is the perfect setting in which to enjoy the superb main desserts. On the ground floor, adjacent to the bar/lounge, there's a sushi bar with its own dessert menu—no, not a predictable scoop of green tea ice cream, but your choice of two tiny cones made from sesame-seed tuiles topped with fruit sorbet, or a sesame-seed pudding served in a small ceramic cylinder, or an exquisite molded kanten that might be flavored with cherry or loquat or pear and white peach. Citarella is an astonishing dessert experience.

# city bakery

❋ *West 18th Street bet. Fifth and Sixth Avenues*
PHONE: 212-366-1414
CREDIT CARDS: AmEx, MC, V
PRICE RANGE: , cookies, $2–3; tarts, $5

The best brownie in New York? The best lemon tart? Fruit tart? Chocolate chip cookie? You don't have to ask many savvy New Yorkers before you'll hear the name City Bakery as their number one choice for any or all of the above.

Ilene Rosen is the chef who carries off this feat on a daily basis. The brownie? It fits most brownie-lovers' idea of nir-vana: thick, dense, chewy, and *echt*-chocolaty. The lemon tart is the subtlest balance of sweet and sour in a just-right-light custard, melty and zingy on the tongue. Among the seasonal fruit tarts, a fall special has cranberries that burst with flavor under an avalanche of brightly caramelized slivered almonds. The melted chocolate cookie is everything the name implies, and should only be ordered if your desire for chocolate recognizes absolutely no boundaries. Even the marshmallows are a homemade glory.

The hum of contented New Yorkers provides most of the atmosphere in this high-ceilinged, industrial-spare Flatiron spot, with cafeteria-style service and seating. Lunchtime is prime time at City Bakery, with a full-tilt takeout crowd vying at the cash registers with tray-toting moms who park their strollers alongside the banquettes. Things quiet down late afternoon through the dinner hour, affording sweets seekers quietude in which to savor their own favorite sugar fixes.

## compass

❋ *208 West 70th Street bet. Amsterdam and West End Avenues*
PHONE: 212-875-8600
CREDIT CARDS: AmEx, MC, V
PRICE RANGE: $8–12

Picture this: A little chocolate dunce cap filled with caramel parfait, towering over three ravioli made from thin, ripe mango slices folded around passionfruit cream, accompanied by fresh coconut tapioca. "Very American," pastry chef Marc Aumont describes it. "My own comfort food."

Not like mother used to make? Maybe not. But mother wasn't Aumont, the young chef at Compass whose exquisite plated desserts are perfectly tuned to the creative pitch of Lincoln Center, a few short blocks south.

In Aumont's hands, staples of New York's dessert world are transformed into creative fantasies. Small cubes of berry gelée, raspberry sour sorbet, vanilla sauce and crumble offer you changing taste-and-texture variations within each spoonful of New York Cheesecake Coupe. Caramel sauce gianduja (almond paste-enriched chocolate) and vanilla ice cream push up the sensations meter on the apple strudel. Vanilla maple ice cream, roasted peanuts, and chocolate sorbet catapult the hot chocolate soufflé way over the top.

No ascetics need apply. These are desserts for the pleasure-loving.

Compass is big in every way, and you can sit where you like: the low table lounge facing the street, its red-banquetted bar, or the sprawling multilevel dining room behind. Stop by pre-performance. Or join the celebs for a post-performance treat. Like its dessert menu, Compass aims to please.

## cones: ice cream artisans
✳ *272 Bleecker Street bet. Jones and Morton Streets*
PHONE: 212-414-1795
CASH ONLY
PRICE RANGE: cones, $3; pints, $9–18; cakes, $25 and $50

Brothers Raul and Oscar D'Aloisio call what they sell ice cream, but it has a rich gelato-like texture similar, they say, to the confection they grew up with as members of the large Italian community in Argentina. They opened Cones in 1998, creating "straight" flavors. "We don't do Chunky Monkey," says Raul. Indeed, Cones's flavors, like strawberry, mango, and canteloupe, are deceptively simple, but pure and rich, as are the outstanding "special flavors" like the best-selling dulce de leche, rum-laced tiramisú, and Marsala-tinged zabaglione, and white chocolate. In 1999 Eric Asimov in the *New York Times* called Cones "some of the best ice cream in the city—rich, smooth, and deeply enough flavored to reawaken taste buds that have forgotten how good ice cream can be." Every year, for a few weeks at the height of the summer, Cones offers the extraordinary Lemon D.P., a reduction of Dom Perignon champagne mixed with lemon sorbet that sells for $18 a pint. Cones also takes special orders for ice cream cakes which the brothers make up on the spot from that day's freshly made ice cream. Cones typically has lines out the door and down the block. Still, says Raul, "New York is not really an ice cream city. In Argentina, there's a gelateria on every block and people are willing to pay more for a good product. Here you have to sell a lot of cones to pay the rent." On our visit, the store was packed and it seemed that New Yorkers were doing their bit, consuming large quantities of the brothers' delectable product, as sort of an ongoing rent party.

## More Exotic Ice Cream Flavors

The Japanese noodle house **Soba-Ya** (229 East 9th St. bet. Second and Third Aves.; 212-533-6966) is the unlikely source of some of the best exotic ice cream flavors in town. We love the sweet-and-pungent honey wasabi, the nutty black sesame, and yuza sorbet, named for the mildly tangy Japanese lime. We differed over the powerful green tea that one of us thought was too bitter, but the other loved. Three flavors to a plate for $5.

# craft

✽ *43 East 19th Street bet. Broadway and Park Avenue South*
PHONE: 212-780-0880
CREDIT CARDS: AmEx, MC, V
PRICE RANGE: pastry, $8; ice creams and sorbet, $4

When Craft opened, it famously discovered that its create-your-own dishes concept was a little too high for most people, and it settled into a more braised-or-grilled norm. Its dessert menu matches the main menu in its reliance on the highest quality in-season ingredients, fresh daily from the greenmarket and select near-city farms. But all the choices are made by pastry chef Karen DeMasco.

This is someone you can trust. Always among her daily choices, we're promised, will be the extraordinary pain perdu, "like the best French toast you've ever tasted," as one guest described it, airy with a hint of sweetness, enhanced by a generous dollop of sautéed apple and caramel ice cream. Doughnuts are also among the unexpected offerings to find their way to first-class menus. Craft's are feathery light, filled with multiple flavors, with sauces for dipping.

On one visit, a chocolate-domed tartuffo filled with hazelnut gelato and surrounded by a pool of potent Nutella sauce was on the menu, as was a single-slice pineapple upside-down cake, as buttery and sweet as our fondest memories.

If the restaurant's name stirs thoughts in you of the Arts and Crafts movement, they're reinforced by the handsome dark woods set against the high beige-toned walls. Think restful—especially at lunch, when the lack of high-rise-office conferencers keeps the decibel level low.

Craft extends itself one door eastward with **Craftbar** (47 East 19th Street, 212-780-0880), a charmingly informal space—cool and dark—with a less-pricey menu that includes desserts by Craft's Karen DeMasco that can be ordered anytime, from noon to midnight ($8). Apple fritters and caramel ice cream is almost always on the menu by popular demand. Her salt-flecked butterscotch pudding is a silken delight, and the brown sugar cake with roasted pineapple and vanilla ice cream is a perfect medley of flavors and textures. Next door to Craftbar (moving right along) is Craft's new sandwich bar, **'wichcraft** (49 East 19th Street, 212-780-0577), a take-out, eat-in place for terrific breakfast and lunch sandwiches and panini ($5–9) and DeMasco's brownies, lemon bars, and "'wich" cookies in chocolate cream and peanut butter versions ($1.50–2).

# edgar's café

✳ *255 West 84th Street bet. Broadway and West End Avenue*
PHONE: 212-496-6126
CASH ONLY
PRICE RANGE: cake slices and tiramisu, $5.25; pies, $4.95; gelato and sorbetto, $5.25

If it's true that Edgar Allen Poe completed "The Raven" in a house on this stretch of Manhattan's West Side (renamed Edgar Allen Poe Street between Broadway and Riverside Drive), we can only hope that the famously melancholy poet had as cozy a cafe to write in as this namesake haunt favored by New York artists, writers, and theater people.

Owner Anna DeLullo has designed it as a faux-bohemian hangout, complete with trompe-l'oeil crumbling stucco walls, old tile and slate floor, marble-topped tables, and cafe chairs with wrought iron backs. Fans of Edgar's know it as one of the city's great dessert destinations, with more than eighty different cakes (at least twelve chocolate varieties), pies, tarts, and other confections—many of them kosher—available at all times along with espresso and cappuccino. A portion of the cakes, such as the berry-laden, sugar-sprinkled Frutti di Bosco tart, are imported from Bindi of Milan. Among the chocolate selections are locally made rich mousse cakes, and the popular chocolate mud and Black Forest cakes. And the tiramisú? Made on premises, this ultra-creamy melange of ladyfingers, espresso, mascarpone, and chocolate is a perfect balance of flavors and textures that, as a bonus, packs a potent rum-kahlua punch. It's simply one of the best we've had in New York.

Weekdays it's a quiet place to read the paper or work at your laptop. Weekends, Edgar's fills up with a brunch crowd ordering French toast, Belgian waffles, and fruit-topped Greek yogurt and rugelach, sugar-free if you like. And at all times, there are snacks and sandwiches that kids love.

# eileen's special cheesecake

✳ *17 Cleveland Place, corner of Kenmare and Centre Streets opposite Lafayette and Spring Streets*
PHONE: 212-966-5585
www.eileenscheesecake.com
CREDIT CARDS: AmEx, Disc, MC, V
PRICE RANGE: single portion, $2.25; 6-inch cakes, $9–13; 10-inch cakes, $22–32

Finding Eileen's is the hard part. But once you've got her coordinates your cheesecake quest is quite possibly over. It depends upon whether you prefer your cheesecake very heavy, or in Eileen's case, very light, almost chiffon-like, with graham-cracker or chocolate-cookie crust and the subtle tang of sour cream. It sounds simple, but Eileen Avezzano's mother's Russian-Jewish recipe, which Eileen started baking twenty-eight years ago, calls for a variation in the preparation of the batter that insures just such a light, silky texture: the eggs are separated, beaten whites are folded into the cream cheese and sour cream base, then the cake is baked slowly in a water bath. The result has won Eileen awards (rated number one by *The Daily News*) and a wide following throughout the city and beyond. ("It's the Dalai Lama's favorite," Eileen reports, "He always sends someone over for it when he's in town.")

We tried four of the twenty-eight flavors—plain, strawberry (most popular), pineapple, and marble—and loved them all. So do many restaurants, Little Italy cafes, and stores around town who regularly sell Eileen's Special Cheesecake, among them Café Biondo, Garden of Eden, and the Amish Market. The cakes are sold, mostly for takeout, from Eileen's glass-fronted shop, which has a few small cafe tables. She offers individually baked single servings, whole cakes in 6- and 10-inch sizes, and 10-inch cake halves. Eileen also ships anywhere in the U.S. Don't worry about the overnight delivery; it's best eaten the next day, she says. We agree.

## The New York Cheesecake Wars

All around the town, you see signs laying claim to "New York's Best Cheesecake." Certainly cheesecake is the dish most closely associated with the city and the one dearest to its sentimental heart. But what is it exactly? And whose really rates the championship title?

Everybody seems to agree on the essentials: cream cheese, sour cream, egg, and lemon, with a graham-cracker crust. And from there? A friend remembers lunching in the 1950s at The Turf, an old-time prime rib house on Broadway that served wedges of cheesecake "so heavy with cream that the narrow end would bend under the weight as it sat on the plate." The Turf is long gone; so is the original Lindy's, a long-time standard-bearer; and so is any cheesecake that quite lives up to that memory of the 1950s.

Today? The **Carnegie Deli's** (854 Seventh Ave. at 55th St., 212-757-2245) version is tall, creamy-dense, and much loved, as is Junior's, even if it is a little shorter and squatter. We're fans of Eileen's Special Cheesecake, a decidedly lighter variant, and so are a multitude of admirers. Then there's a lemon-flavored version made especially for **Café Liebowitz** which is outstanding and a must-try for purists. Latin-inflected contenders include the slightly tart guava cheesecake at **Mary's off Jane** and **Bruno Bakery's** ricotta-based dulce de leche. Both **Martha Frances Mississippi Cheesecake** and **Terrance Brennan's** serve up a superb southern-style praline version.

And the winner is. . .?

## elephant & castle

❊ *68 Greenwich Avenue bet. Seventh Avenue South and West 11th Street*
PHONE: 212-243-1400
CREDIT CARDS: AmEx, MC, V
PRICES: crepes, $4.75–6.75; other, $4.50–8

In the 1970s crepes were in, then they were out, now they're in again; and all the while Elephant & Castle has stayed the course, retaining all its famous, now retro specialties, of which crepes were and are prime. The Grand Marnier version stands in for an after-dinner drink; Casablanca is a harmony of vanilla ice cream, banana, and hot fudge; Chestnut crepe parisienne is a recent addition in which French chestnut puree is deliciously embellished with apricot essence and whipped cream. Then there are those other Castle classics: Boston Indian pudding, whose "secret recipe" of slow-cooked cornmeal and molasses is a veritable time machine for rock-bound yankees; carrot cake that won a "best in New York" twenty years ago (it's holding up nicely); hot fudge sundaes made with Valrhona chocolate; and of course, frou frou, fresh seasonal fruit with Greek yogurt drizzled with Greek honey (made by monks in Crete) or a more secular Vermont maple syrup. Innovations at the Castle include Ciao Bella sorbets and bananas Foster served with sautéed fresh strawberries. Far out.

## eleven madison park

✳ *11 Madison Avenue at 24th Street*
PHONE: 212-889-0905
CREDIT CARDS: AmEx, Disc, MC, V
PRICE RANGE: most desserts, $10; chocolate soufflé, $24

At Eleven Madison Park, the dessert specialty is the chocolate soufflé for two. And it's the real thing: a great cloud of flavor that has crept up to form a puffy dome, collapsing at the touch of a spoon, here luxuriously enriched with a creamy fudge sauce ladled in by your server. You'll have to wait thirty minutes. Wonderful. There are few dining rooms in New York we'd rather wait in. This former MetLife lobby space is elegant and airy, with its vast windows and majestic marble walls softened by towering masses of flowers, a sea of gleaming napery, and the original bronze chandeliers overhead. If you're in the raised bar-lounge area, all is spread out below you with a vista of Madison Square Park outside the windows.

The soufflé is not on the menu, but we're assured it's always available if you know to ask. Then again, you may be too taken with pastry chef Nicole Kaplan's ever-changing menu to care. One day it may be a lemon assiette, an individual lemon soufflé set off by the contrasting intensities of a macaroon and a sorbet. Chocolate caramel tart, the kind of dessert well-brought-up adults claim they can "only eat a bite of," is outrageously accompanied by roasted bananas and peanut fudge ice cream. Dark chocolate dome? Don't ask. Even a plate of cookies and cakes, the kind of pussy-footing finale we usually scorn, is a many-splendored sensation.

One well-kept secret: Eleven Madison Park keeps that high and handsome lounge area open straight through the afternoon for light bites and desserts. Play hooky and go; for an hour or so you'll feel you're one of Manhattan's most privileged insiders.

# fauchon

❋ *Swissotel—The Drake New York, 442 Park Avenue at 56th Street*
PHONE: 212-308-5919
CREDIT CARDS: AmEx, MC, V

❋ *1000 Madison Avenue at 77th Street*
PHONE: 212-570-2211

❋ *1383 Third Avenue bet. 78th and 79th Streets*
PHONE: 212-517-9600

When Fauchon, the venerable nineteenth-century Parisian purveyor of fancy foods, teas, chocolates, and pastries, finally opened in New York in 2000 (the firm has 750 outlets in 33 countries), the city's dessert quotient spiked as high as Mont Blanc, which happens to be the highest of the French Alps and also the name of one of the great commemorative patis- serie creations in the French canon. (Another is the delicious Paris-Brest, a round—that is, wheel-shaped—mocha-filled éclair named for the famous bicycle race.) Executive pastry chef Florian Bellenger is in charge of preparing the roster of Fauchon's classic cakes, tarts, cookies, viennoiseries, ice creams, and sorbets, all of which are available at the glittering Park Avenue location—a combination gourmet emporium and tea room of relaxed elegance.

To enjoy pastries, as we did, in the tea room, is to immerse oneself in the French experience. The table is laid with Limoges china on a spotless white cloth, forks placed tines down in European style; Fauchon's signature pink and gold motif is carried through from the awning at the entrance to the upholstery on the blond-wood armchairs and recamier sofas; and a gilt mural with the names of famous teas provides a backdrop. In France pastries are traditionally eaten at break- fast (Fauchon's pain au chocolat is baked with two bars of chocolate inside) or tea time, so it's logical that a full after- noon tea is offered (mini sandwiches, canapés, and desserts). But, on a first visit, it's more fun to first goggle at the many pastries in the shop's cases, make a very difficult decision on what to order (we recommend the Paris-Brest and fresh berries Charlotte), then repair to the tea room where you can enjoy your dessert with either a pot of one of the many teas, coffee, hot chocolate, or a selection of iced teas, juices, nectars, and waters. Afterward, wander through the store to view an entire wall of 115 teas, and cases filled with Fauchon's amazing candied fruits, more than forty types of mustard, and much more.

Fauchon's Madison Avenue location, the site of the late lamented Sant Ambroeus tea room, has a cappuccino bar and plenty of pastries, but for the full Mont Blanc, Park Avenue's the ticket.

## When Dessert is a Very Special Cake

Whether for weddings or birthdays or other special occasions, a gorgeous or amazingly decorated cake is often at the top of the want list (and should probably be in the pre-nup). Many bakeries discussed in this book will oblige with fabulous, custom-made creations—Payard and Fauchon spring to mind, along with Black Hound, and Cupcake Café. But here are more New York specialty bakers whose artistry with sugar and buttercream can interpret your wildest or most romantic fantasies: **Alba Italian Pastry Shoppe** (7001 18th Ave., Brooklyn; 718-232-2122; www.albapastry.com) for their skill with marzipan decoration and range of different cake fillings, including ricotta cheese and cassata cream. **Colette's Cakes** (681 Washington Street bet. West 10th and Charles Sts.; 212-366-6530; www.colettescakes.com) for whimsical designs and finishes. **Creative Cakes** (400 East 74th St. bet. First and Second Avenues; 212-794-9811) for funky and fun conversation pieces. **Sylvia Weinstock Cakes** (273 Church Street bet. Franklin and Watts St.; 212-925-6698; www.sylviaweinstockcakes.com) for magnificent cakes with the most convincing trompe-l'oeil flowers. Most bakers are by appointment only for special orders.

See websites where possible for examples and prices, and for additional listings look into *City Weddings* by Joan Hamburg.

# financier patisserie

❋ *62 Stone Street*
PHONE: 212-344-5600
CREDIT CARDS: AmEx, MC, V
PRICE RANGE: pastries, $2.25–3.75; cakes, $24.50–38

When a French gourmet enters a patisserie for the first time, he orders an éclair. The theory is, if the éclair is good, everything else will be, too.

The éclairs at Financier (pronounced "fee-NAHN-cee-ay")—one an intense coffee cream in pâte-à-choux pastry with a sticky glaze of caramel running its length—are among New York's very best. The same can be said for all the twenty-five or thirty choices spread before your dazzled eyes: A religieuse, seldom seen and never forgotten. Small strawberry passionfruit cakes with the strawberries nestled in the mousse. A plum tart, its fresh plums resting on buttercream beneath a crumbly top. "The best macaroons I've ever had," in one friend's words. And with your coffee comes a miniature financier (shaped like a little gold brick, hence the name), an irresistible almond sponge cake that the patisserie also sells a few thousand of each week.

Chef Eric Bedoucha prides himself on his adherence to classic standards, with perhaps the smallest concessions to his own tastes. (The layers of coffee buttercream, chocolate ganache, and almond sponge cake beneath a deep chocolate glaze in his opera stand perhaps 1/8-inch higher than their French ancestors, he admits.)

With its immaculate appointments—tile flooring, pastel walls, comfortable faux bamboo chairs—Financier would fit into any smart European street, from Paris to Rome to Copenhagen. All the more wonder that it's in Manhattan's financial district, on a hard-to-find cobblestoned street near Hanover Square.

Seats at the few tables fill quickly with lunchers enjoying one of the day's un-deli sandwiches or salads. But with the doors open 7 a.m. to 6 p.m. (to 4 p.m. on Saturdays), you have lots of options. For a patisserie picnic, South Ferry Park and Battery Park are a few minutes' walk away.

## good enough to eat

❋ *483 Amsterdam Avenue bet. 83rd and 84th Streets*
PHONE: 212-496-0163
CREDIT CARDS: AmEx, MC, V
PRICE RANGE: cake slices, $5.50; pie slices, $5; brownies, squares, and cookies, $1.75–3.75

"We bake all day and all night," says Carrie Levin, chef and owner of this homey neighborhood restaurant known for bountiful breakfasts and classic all-American food at lunch and dinner as well. The pastry case is filled with chocolate, carrot, and coconut layer cakes; fruit, pumpkin, and pecan pies; crisps, squares, brownies, and cookies—in short, all the comfy desserts Levin remembers from childhood. But, she learned her baking skills in Brussels, where her parents lived for a time in her youth. "It's where the best bakeries are," says Levin, who uses only Belgian chocolate, and on Tuesday nights prepares a special Belgian dessert: orange-almond-Grand Marnier cake.

In 1981 Levin opened Good Enough, dedicating her restaurant to "good, old-fashioned American food." Her baked goods, made with the assistance of Michelle Weber, have an avid following. One customer, who comes in regularly for a slice of Levin's scrumptious coconut layer cake with rich cream cheese frosting showered with shredded coconut, was so upset when Levin once changed the filling to lemon custard that the original recipe was immediately reinstated. Another neighborhood denizen calls the strawberry pie "to die for" and we found the pumpkin smooth and perfectly textured. If there's any doubt that New Yorkers need home-style desserts now more than ever, Levin points to the fact that after September 11, 2001, her weekly flour order increased from 700 to 1,000 pounds.

## grand central market

**Grand Central Terminal, Main Concourse and Dining Concourse**

✳ *Lexington Avenue at 43rd Street*
PHONE: 212-340-2347

The street-level arcade starts at the Lexington Avenue and 43rd Street end of the station with **Corrado** (212-599-4321), where you'll find pastries ($4–4.50), whole cakes ($19–25), tea cakes ($2.50), and cookies from fine bakeries including Balthazar (see main entry), Dumas, Eleni's, and others. **Zaro's** has many fresh-looking whole cakes ($12.95–15.95), including carrot, cheese, and fruit tortes, but slices only at their shop near Track 34.

On the lower dining concourse only **Junior's** (212-983-5257) provides a full-service restaurant where you can get a sit-down meal and of course the famous cheesecake in all nine variations and sizes (Little Fella-size cheesecake is $2.95). **Custard Beach** (212-983-9155) is the place for real frozen custard made with extra egg yolk in a continuous-flow machine; four main daily flavors (possibly crème brûlée or dulche de leche), guilt-free since this custard is 90 percent fat-free. You can also get sugar-free frozen yogurt, sorbets, smoothies, and Belgian waffles, freshly made throughout the day. Price range: $2.75–4.20. **Little Pie Company**'s scrumptious pies, individual cheesecakes, and tea cakes available at its other branches, are here to be sampled.





# houston's

❋ *378 Park Avenue South at 27th Street*

PHONE: 212-689-1090

CREDIT CARDS: AmEx, MC, V

PRICE RANGE: $8

Looking for a pleasant, out-of-New-York-like American experience? Houston's is just the destination—a non-edgy oasis that feels positively Midwestern compared to its flashier, trendier Park Avenue South neighbors.

One reason is that this Houston's is a branch of the successful restaurant chain that stretches across the continent. If they have a formula, it's one a lot of New Yorkers have taken to their hearts. (Lines can be long at peak hours.)

For starters, Houston's couldn't be friendlier, with staffers who'll seat and serve you with a smile—even if you order just dessert. The bonus: Everyone, not just your designated wait person, watches out for you. The atmosphere is more relaxed lounge than bustling eatery: dim light, deep colors, and lots of snuggly booths and wraparound banquettes available to all. (One unworldly couple, babe in arms, got prime seating when we visited.)

The desserts are a perfect fit. Beyond some Edy's ice cream, they number just three, each a perfectly executed version of an American classic. We went for the key lime pie enthusiastically recommended by friends, but that's strictly a summer special. Always on the menu is the many-splendored five-nut brownie, with vanilla ice cream, gussied up with a creamy champagne sauce. The cheesecake is tall and smo-o-o-th. Apple crumble is buttery, with the balance happily tilting toward more walnuts than most restaurateurs want to shell out for.

Like every Houston's, this one has its own dedicated dessert chef in the kitchen, baking with prime ingredients. Chain? It's a far cry from bearded colonels and golden arches.

### houston's citygroup center

❋ *153 E. 53rd Street at Lexington Avenue*

PHONE: 212-888-3828

Same menu. Same smiling service. To our minds a little less welcoming in its below-ground location. But don't let that hold you back. The happy throngs don't seem to mind at all.

## hungarian pastry shop

❋ *1030 Amsterdam Avenue at 111th Street*

PHONE: 212-866-4230

CASH ONLY

PRICE RANGE: pastries and slices, $1.75–2.75; whole cakes, $25 and up

Walk a few steps inside the door and it's not hard to imagine you've time-traveled back to a student cafe near the university in Old Budapest: plain wooden tables and chairs worn with age in the low-ceilinged room in back, the low hum of students debating art and philosophy and cybergenetics. Cybergenetics? Well, these students are from Columbia, just up Amsterdam Avenue, and this is one of their hangouts.

Hungarian Pastry Shop is one of the last places in New York offering the full range of indigenous Hungarian desserts, along with the specialties it shares with its European neighbors: hearty strudels (in four varieties), Linzertorte, Sacher torte, Dobostorte, Stefania, goosefoot cake—all listed above the counter where you place your order and pick up your food. It's not fancy, but it's authentic. Budapest-trained chef Zoltan Bona uses all butter, along with quality ingredients that he gathers through his own sources, like the poppyseeds oozing from the overfilled poppyseed strudel, and the cocoa and chocolate that combine to make a blissful Rigo Janci.

It all makes the perfect ending to a mini-*mittel European* outing: an amble around Columbia's lovely campus or Morningside Park—then a relaxing sojourn at one of Hungarian Pastry Shop's sidewalk tables, gazing at the soaring spires of the Cathedral of St. John the Divine, just across the avenue. Total cost: less than $10. Ah, Budapest.

## itzocan cafe

※ *438 East 9th Street bet. First Avenue and Avenue A*
PHONE: 212-677-5856
CASH ONLY
PRICE RANGE: entrees, $9.50–14.50; desserts, $4.50

This tiny, fourteen-seat, BYO Mexican restaurant is not your average burrito and guacamole house (although the freshly made guacamole, salsa, and homemade chips are outstanding).

The food, under the direction of owner-chef Anselmo Bello and his brother Adolfo (a third brother, Fermin, cooks too), is distinctly a cut above, even innovative, and that includes desserts. The thing is, the dessert menu is often subject to change, so call ahead to ask if Bello's much-in-demand molten chocolate mole cake with caramel sauce is on that night. Before opening Itzocan in July 2002, Bello worked in several French restaurants and he brings the knowledge he gained to many exciting fusion dishes, both entrees and desserts. The dining room's Aztec motifs and Bello's own hand-painted ceramics provide a perfect setting in which to enjoy burrito-type bistro fare or well-priced entrees, followed by the mole cake or one of the daily specials, such as a marvelous tres leches cake soaked in the three sweet milks and doused with Mexican chocolate sauce, or a semolina flan, or a profiterole, or a French-style frangipane fruit tart with a grating of Oaxacan chocolate. You can come just for dessert, but—as at any restaurant without a bar or lounge—not during the busy dinner hours, when you're likely to be asked to wait outside for the next available table. The food and the friendly, well-informed waiters make the wait eminently worthwhile.

## Tres Leches Cake

It seems to be cropping up everywhere in endless variations, this cake soaked with three kinds of sweetened milks—evaporated, sweetened condensed, and sometimes cream. Often you find it with a meringue topping, sometimes chocolate, sometimes plain, but they're all called by the same name. We asked Roberto Santibanez, culinary director of **Rosa Mexicano** (61 Columbus Ave. at 62nd St., 212-977-7700), what he knew of its origins. "Every Latin American country knows about it," he said, pointing out that it's become so popular that in Mexico City there are cake stores dedicated solely to tres leches. Santibanez believes that it was not originally a Latin recipe. Because tres leches cake is not remembered in Mexico before the 1950s or '60s, Santibanez suspects that the recipe may have been introduced by a condensed milk company around that time as a promotion. Wherever it came from, it caught on, appealing to the famous Latin sweet tooth, and today even upscale restaurants like Rosa Mexicano offer it. At the Lincoln Center location, tres leches is served in a chocolate-rum version topped with vanilla ice cream and served with sugared bananas. We discovered an excellent plain version, served simply with a cinnamon stick and fresh mint, at **Mexicana Mama** (525 Hudson St. bet. Charles and West 10th Sts.), a tiny, very popular West Village restaurant, where you can order it at the tiny bar or get it to go.

# il laboratorio del gelato

✤ *95 Orchard Street at Delancey*
PHONE: 212-343-9922
CASH ONLY
PRICE RANGE: small cup, $3.25; large cup, $3.75;
pints, $4.75, two or more pints, $4.50 each

Jon Snyder founded Ciao Bella (see listing) when he was only nineteen, worked hard, got burned out, and at age twenty-five sold the company to enter the world of high finance. Happy ending: In August 2002 Snyder abandoned the financial world and returned for a second act with Laboratorio, dedicated, as Ciao Bella had been, to New York-based, high quality, small-batch gelato and sorbet. The new company operates out of

Laboratorio's sizable Lower East Side kitchen—fronted by a tiny blue-and-white gelateria cafe—just steps from the Tenement Museum. You can walk in and sample any one of a dozen outstanding, rotating flavors—a bright, nutty hazelnut, perhaps, or pistachio, or an intensely fruity pear sorbet—along with Divini, packages of four or a dozen gelato truffles in raspberry, dark chocolate, and chocolate walnut covered with exquisitely crunchy coatings (white chocolate sprinkles, crunchy hazelnuts, and coconut) that can be rushed home in insulated bags guaranteed to keep the delectable morsels frozen for up to forty minutes, or consumed on the spot. A selection of ten basic flavors is also available in 18-ounce packages in gourmet markets such as Citarella, Grace's Marketplace, Dean & DeLuca, and Tuller Premium Foods in Cobble Hill, Brooklyn. Laboratorio is also served in over seventy-five New York restaurants including Pastis, Mary's Fish Camp, Five Points, Red Cat, Baldoria, and Barbaluc. So there is no excuse for not trying Snyder's increasingly ubiquitous and superb new product. The inevitable question: How does it differ from the still excellent Ciao Bella? Mainly in the intensity of the new small-batch flavors like milk chocolate, ginger, caramel, and Pear William (brandy) gelatos and fruit-based sorbets like nectarine, tangerine, and mango, all using local ingredients as much as possible.

~~~~~~~~~~~~~~~~~~~~~~~~~~~~~~~~~~~~~~~~~~~~~

## jacques torres chocolate

❖ *66 Water Street, Brooklyn*
PHONE: 718-875-9772
CREDIT CARDS: AmEx, MC, V
PRICE RANGE: pastries (available Saturdays only), $2.50; chocolates, $16–43 per pound

Time for a detour? For this one, you'll have to leave the sky-scraper groves of Manhattan. But barely. Walk or cycle across the Brooklyn Bridge some nice Saturday. As you exit, double back to the right, toward the water. Just before you reach River Café at Fulton Ferry Landing, veer right into Water Street. There, among the slowly gentrifying warehouses of Brooklyn's Dumbo district, you'll hit the end of the chocolate rainbow: Jacques Torres Chocolate.

Every weekday morning, you can sip some of the best hot chocolate in any borough, along with the flakiest of crois-sants and pains au chocolat. But on Saturdays only, the pastry chef who dazzled the glitterati at Le Cirque for eleven years abandons his current role of chocolatier extraordinaire and returns to his roots. For this one day, he makes whatever pas-tries strike his fancy. Not one or two, but lots. And not only chocolate-based. If you're lucky, he'll be serving up a *pithivier*, the ethereally rich puff pastry tart filled with almond cream. We shared a gold-standard wedge of plum tart.

As for chocolate? Ooh-la-la! Brownies so rich they have their own bank account. A crinkly-layered chocolate napoleon that will make you lick the paper afterward. A light chocolate-custard éclair. Everything just out of the kitchen that's visible through a glass wall of the gem-like shop. You may snag a seat at one of the few tables and chairs. (As we write, Torres plans an expansion.) Or take your booty with you and picnic at Fulton Ferry Landing's small park, or the meadow-like Empire Park up to its right. Calories? No problem. Walk them off on your way home.

# le pain quotidien

* *100 Grand Street bet. Mercer and Greene Streets*
  PHONE: 212-625-9009
* *19th Street bet. Broadway and Park Avenue*
  *South (inside ABC Carpet & Home)*
  PHONE: 212-673-7900
* *833 Lexington Avenue bet. 63rd and 64th Streets*
  PHONE: 212-755-5810
* *1336 First Avenue at 72nd Street*
  PHONE: 212-717-4800
* *50 West 72nd bet. Central Park West and*
  *Columbus Avenue*
  PHONE: 212-712-9700
* *1131 Madison Avenue bet. 84th and 85th Streets*
  PHONE: 212-327-4900
  CREDIT CARDS: AmEx, MC, V
  PRICE RANGE: small tarts, $5–9; large tarts, $14–24

This Belgian coffee house chain, with thirty locations throughout Europe, is known for excellent breads (the name means "daily bread"), but also for cakes and pastries, most of which are baked at the Mercer Street kitchen for its New York outlets. Executive Chef Ari Cohen presides over everything from baguettes, rolls, and croissants to organic vegan muffins, airy Belgian-style brownies, almond pound cake with orange peel, an intense chocolate espresso tart, and the subtle chestnut-cream-filled Mont Blanc with a chocolate truffle hidden in the center. At Pain Quotidien the atmosphere is rustic European. Customers sit at long communal farmhouse tables to enjoy soups, sandwiches, salads, and of course dessert, confident that almost all ingredients used, from flours to locally grown fruits, are organic and that famed Belgian chocolate is used exclusively. The SoHo location features a spectacular glass wall that separates the front counter from the dining room, a dramatic space that can be reserved for special occasions.

new york's 50+ best places to enjoy dessert

# lifethyme

❊ *410 Sixth Avenue bet. 8th and 9th Streets*
PHONE: 212-420-9099
CREDIT CARDS: AmEx, MC, V
PRICE RANGE: cookies, $2.25 and up; cake slices, $3.95 and up; pies or cheesecake, $4.25 and up; whole cakes, $45 and up

Business is brisk at the LifeThyme bakery counter, and the customers know what they like. "What's good?" we asked on our first visit of a guy who was waiting for his order. "The Toll Booth," he said pointing reflexively to what looked like an oversize chocolate chip cookie. "And the truffle brownie," he continued, indicating rich cocoa-dusted, chocolaty looking squares,"and the muffins are great, and the Black Out cake, and the lemon and orange cakes are very good." We were writing furiously as he left and two young women, who'd been listening to the list, volunteered that actually the chocolate-chocolate chip cookie was best. At that point, Camillo Sabella, the youthful chief baker appeared, ready to talk to us about the many strictly vegan (no butter, no dairy) desserts he prepares every day. The strawberry cheesecake, which looked tempting, was, he said, made with tofu. "It's imitation cream cheese," he commented, at which point a distinguished looking gentlemen who'd just ordered a piece said, "I take exception to that!" as he didn't consider it imitation anything.

That's exactly the point with good vegan baking today, a far cry from the bad old days when pallid, tasteless confections elicited more nose wrinkling than lip smacking. At LifeThyme, Sabella develops recipes aiming for the lightness he remembers in the desserts he grew up with. As a result the texture of his vegan cheesecake is closer to the lovely loose-curd Sicilian-style ricotta versions we love than most of the real thing we've found around town. Sabella's has a nut and oat crust and silken tofu filling with lemon zest and juice, cinnamon, vanilla, and fresh organic strawberries and preserves. The rich truffle brownie, made of organic chocolate, cocoa powder, and, for the chocolate glaze, silken tofu, is a winner, as is the richly caramelized pineapple upside-down cake—moist with the fresh fruit and its juices that soak and sweeten the crumb during baking. Sabella often makes elaborate tiered wedding cakes and also offers a large repertoire of holiday cakes and pastries—pies with a wheat-free spelt crust, hamentaschen, rugelach, and strudel—all of which are kosher. He sells about two-hundred Toll Booth cookies a day at $2.25 a pop, and yes, it's a wonderful cookie, crammed with organic chocolate chips and roasted pecan halves lightly bound together with spelt flour and cane-juice sweetener that doesn't set off sugar alarms in the brain. No, you don't have to be vegan to enjoy LifeThyme.

Other places to enjoy vegan baking include **Integral Yoga Foods** (229 West 13th St. bet. 7th and 8th Aves., 212-243-2642); **Healthy Pleasures** (93 University Place bet. 11th and 12th Sts., 212-353-3663); and see listings in this book for **Angelica Kitchen**, **Quintessence**, and **Teany**.

# l'impero

Tudor City has long been one of the city's hidden wonders—a hilltop fortress of sedate brick apartment buildings surrounding their own central park. Now there's an extra inducement to search it out: A stellar neo-Italian restaurant, L'Impero, with one of the city's top pastry chefs turning out equally stellar desserts.

For chef Heather Carlucci-Rodriguez, Italian is just the jumping-off place for the stunning collages of taste, texture, and color she assembles on a plate: a Spanish-inspired chocolate olive-oil mousse snuggles up to a vanilla custard-filled bavarese, with grappa-caramelized bananas and a swirl of whipped cream. Yogurt semifreddo, a honey-roasted peach, and sesame baklava are a plated symphony of crunchy and smooth, of frothy and dense, of sweet and tart.

Everything changes based on what the season yields. One creation looks as though it will, by popular demand, remain forever, a chocolate "soup" in which crème fraiche pannacotta, walnut financier, rum zabaglione, and espresso granita begin life alone, then marry into a spectrum of changing flavor sensations.

The bar area and lounge where desserts are served is comfortable, with a subtly backlit bar to color your experience. Pause on the iron-railed walkway over 42nd Street to admire the East River vista as you leave. Life can be beautiful.

# link

❊ *120 East 15th Street corner of Irving Place*

PHONE: 212-995-1010

CREDIT CARDS: AmEx, MC, V

PRICE RANGE: desserts, $6.50; fondue for two, $12;
entrées, $14–19.50

Union Square's newest culinary star is Julian Clauss-Ehlers—formerly executive chef at the Moroccan-inflected Zitoune—who directs the kitchen at the trendy new restaurant/bar/lounge Link. Located on a short, lively block of no less than four theaters, and opposite Irving Plaza, Link attracts both the pre- and post-theater crowds, as well as neighborhood regulars. Clauss-Ehlers's lunch and dinner menus offer satisfying bistro fare, along with *amuse-bouche* (little bites before the meal), and of course, a selection of outstanding desserts. Link's ultra-cool design in a palette of brown, blue, and gold makes for a relaxing environment, especially in the spacious lounge ringed by banquettes and furnished with velvet-upholstered cube-shaped ottomans and low tables. There, with votive lights twinkling on tables and in wall niches, we sampled two of the chef's most popular and delicious desserts. The warm, baked fruit-and-nut Moroccan b'steeya is a flaky phyllo-dough pastry (resembling a turnover) filled with plump rum-soaked raisins, almonds, and spices and sprinkled with cinnamon and sugar. It's served with two spoons of ginger ice cream, in case you want to share, but it's so good, you may end up fighting over it. We also enjoyed warm banana bread pudding served with an intense griottine cherry coulis and homemade vanilla ice cream—about as comforting as a dessert gets. Other dessert selections include a very popular chocolate-chestnut-mousse creation "enrobed in a bittersweet chocolate" and served with Armangnac anglaise. Clauss-Ehlers's appealing summer dessert menu features English summer pudding with crème fraiche, and—what a brilliant idea—a piña colada ice cream soda (with rum if you like).

Chef Clauss-Ehlers is also in charge at Link's adjoining 3 Square, a cafe and food shop that offers some of the best takeout in the city: pot pies, quiches, sandwiches, salads, pastas, and more are always available, as are many patisserie selections that include mousse cake, carrot cake, strawberry shortcakes, rich brownies, hefty chocolate-dipped macaroons, fruit bars, and cookies, all made on premises. PRICE RANGE: cake slices, $2.25–3; whole cakes, $13.50–42.

## little pie company

❉ *407 West 14th Street bet. Ninth and Tenth Avenues*
PHONE: 212-736-4780

❉ *424 West 43rd Street bet. Ninth and Tenth Avenues*
PHONE: 212-414-2324

❉ *Grand Central Terminal, lower-level dining concourse*
PHONE: 212-983-3538
www.littlepiecompany.com
CREDIT CARDS: AmEx, Disc, MC, V
PRICE RANGE: 5-inch pies, $5; pie slices, $3.50; cake slices, $5; 10-inch pies, $16–25; 8-inch pies, $10–15; cakes, $4–25

There are three sizes of pie here, 10-inch, 8-inch, and the 5-inch "little" pie that gives the company its name. These one- or (rarely) two-person pies are offered in almost every one of LPC's ten pie variations, of which we tested: cherry, sour cream apple walnut, Mississippi mud, key lime, and banana cream. Most of the fruit pies use an old-fashioned crust made with a combination of butter and lard for an extremely flaky result. (An all-butter crust will not be as flaky.) The cherry pie was wonderfully light, deeply filled with slightly tart, bright pink Montmorency cherries from an orchard in upstate New York. Made without cornstarch thickener, it could scarcely have had a better cherry flavor and overall texture. The sour cream apple walnut is sweet and chunky, made with a butter-apple cider-cinnamon crust filled with thinly sliced, layered Granny Smith apples and sour cream and topped with a rich brown sugar and nut streusel. Warmed up, with a scoop of vanilla ice cream, it would satisfy the most extreme sweet tooth. The same goes for the Mississippi mud pie that doesn't bother to look pretty because it doesn't have to: a hardened chocolate glaze paves over a brownie streusel and a cookie crust. The key lime was smooth and intense, made with sweetened condensed milk and cream and a graham-cracker crust. Finally, we tried the banana cream coconut pie, made with LPC's light and flaky dough (that uses vegetable short-ening) and found it to be a heavenly little mouth-melter topped with a cloud of sweetened whipped cream. LPC also makes old-fashioned cakes (applesauce carrot, yellow, choco-late, pound cakes, cheesecake, cupcakes, and loaf cakes, plus seasonal pies—pumpkin, pecan, etc.) that can be enjoyed at the store with espresso, cappuccino, or a latte, or gift-pack-aged and shipped to your best friend.

# martha frances mississippi cheesecake

✣ *1707 Second Avenue bet. 88th and 89th Streets*
PHONE: 212-360-0900
CREDIT CARDS: AmEx, MC, V
PRICE RANGE: cake slices, $4.25–4.95; cakes, $40–42;
pies, $20–26

This little bakery cafe next door to trendy Elaine's is a trove of southern specialties that has New Yorkers lining up through the day and into the night (it's open till midnight Thursday, Friday, and Saturday). A typical midnight-snack order might be a slice of white chocolate cheesecake; bread pudding with chocolate chips and hot bourbon sauce; and maybe some sugar cookies with cream cheese icing. Owner Jan Boscarino, a native of Jackson, Mississippi, bakes everything but the cheesecakes herself, using old family recipes for the likes of caramel cake, delta fudge pie, banana chocolate cream pie, and key lime pie on a daily basis. The dozen varieties of what she calls "embellished New York cheesecake"—based on her mother Martha Frances's recipe—are baked for her in Jackson and shipped to New York. A rich cream cheese base and graham-cracker crust is wonderfully tasty plain or in any of the rich variations, including deeply Southern praline, understandably a best-seller. "I have the nicest customers in New York," says Boscarino, who believes that "good desserts make people act sweet." Even the notoriously snappish customers from Elaine's, it seems, often end their evenings at Martha Frances's sidewalk cafe, mellowing out with cake and cappuccino.

# mary's off jane bakery

*❋ 34 Eighth Avenue bet. Jane and West Twelfth Streets (a few blocks south of 14th Street)*

PHONE: 212-243-5972

www.marysoffjane.com

CREDIT CARDS: AmEx, MC, V

PRICE RANGE: desserts, $1.25–4.25; cakes, $28 and up

Mary Arda's bakery cafe opened in 2002 offering an intriguing mix of American favorites and Latin-inflected specialties. So if you're in the mood either for a slice of moist Devil's Food cake or a mojito cookie (a tangy-sweet hockey puck-sized shortbread with lime icing, whose name and flavor refer to the ubiquitous cocktail) Mary's off Jane can satisfy the yen. Arda's Cuban-Brazilian heritage provided her with the basis for many traditional recipes but she's also developed her own versions of standards that make for interesting fusion flavors. Her coconut layer cake, for example, has a smooth dulce de leche cream filling. Guava, the tangy pink tropical fruit that non-Latin New Yorkers are learning to love, is featured in the classic Brazilian "Romeo and Juliet," so called because the pastry's two filling ingredients—guava and cream cheese—go together as perfectly as Shakespeare's young lovers. There's much more to enjoy on the international menu, while sipping either cappuccino or Mexican chili-enhanced hot chocolate or passionfruit lemonade. Painted in bright tropical colors, Mary's off Jane provides a cheerful, inviting place in which to relax and relish desserts like South Florida pineapple upside-down cake, fall fruit cobbler, or a "Boston Cream" custard-filled heirloom cake draped with dark chocolate ganache. There's flan too, in flavors that change daily, and—great idea!—a brûléed lemon bar. Mary Arda and Daniella Binder make everything on premises, aiming, says Arda, for homestyle appeal for the sophisticated palate.

# mondrian

✳ *1026 Third Avenue bet. 60th and 61st Streets*
PHONE: 212-759-8730
www.mondrianpastry.com
CREDIT CARDS: AmEx, MC, V
PRICE RANGE: traditional pastries, $4; small tarts, $5.75;
artist-named pastries, $6; whole cakes $20–50

Outside of the Met, or the Art Show, this is the only place in Manhattan you are likely to find Picasso, Matisse, Renoir, Miro, Monet, Michelangelo, Rodin, Gauguin, and of course, Mondrian under one roof. But the art in question is not a mere visual treat, it's delicious too, composed of chocolate, spices, caramel, fruits, nuts, rich creams, and more, all artfully transformed into exquisite mini-sculptures. At first, you don't really want to destroy these creations by biting into them; but then you do and, voilà, you've become one with the art—or the tart, as the case may be. Two of the most popular pastries are the Mondrian, a suitably streamlined caramel-coated oval of hazelnut streusel, spicy caramel cream, and chocolate sponge spread with caramel marmalade, and meringue mousse; and the Michelangelo, a soufflé-like chocolate chiboust filled with raspberry jam and praline crunch and encircled by fresh raspberries. They're all the creations of artist-pastry chef Michel Willaume, an award-winning expatriot Parisian. His rather spare, narrow modernist shop-cafe has a few tables where you can sit and enjoy espresso and fancy pastry, but also danishes, pain au chocolat, brioche, savories, and sandwiches. There are handmade chocolate bonbons too—also gorgeously designed—along with delicate French macaroons, petits fours, and tuiles. Special-occasion cakes are a Mondrian specialty, made as elaborate as dreams allow. Log on to the website for a bonus recipe for a chocolate tart you can make at home.

# nl

❊ *169 Sullivan Street bet. Bleecker and*
*Houston Streets*
PHONE: 212-387-8801
CREDIT CARDS: AmEx, MC, V
PRICE RANGE: pancakes, $5–8

The afternoon we came to NL (the name is the abbreviation for the Netherlands), the sun was warming the umbrella-shaded outdoor tables and we felt like we were on a deck in some other country. It might as well have been Holland, because we were eating and enjoying sweet Dutch pancakes with maple syrup and vanilla butter courtesy of chef Nathan Kendel, who serves them up in six other delicious variations, including plain with sugar and lemon, with banana and chocolate, with Nutella, and with vanilla ice cream and orange sauce. Something between a crepe and an American pancake, NL's pancakes are the size of a dinner plate, one per serving, and slightly fluffy.

Yes, you could eat them for breakfast, but the Dutch-converted New Yorkers love them for dessert, especially in this restaurant's brightly attractive surroundings—orange velour banquettes; fresh red tulips on the bar; a blue and white tile back wall that is a modernist nod toward Delft. As we chatted with chef Kendel, examining the restaurant's appealing neo-European menu, he told us of another Dutch treat—poffertjes, which are little puffed-up cakes (each about the size of an American fifty-cent piece) that are cooked in a special Dutch cast-iron mold, then served piled on a plate like little pillows sprinkled with powdered sugar, drizzled with strawberry sauce and dots of vanilla buttercream. Would he cook them for us? Sure, he said, come back tomorrow; we did, and counted the dish as our second Dutch discovery in a week.

# once upon a tart

❊ *135 Sullivan Street bet. Houston and Prince Streets*
PHONE: 212-387-8869
CREDIT CARDS: AmEx, Disc, MC, V
PRICE RANGE: small tarts, $5–5.50; savories, $5.50;
7-inch fruit tarts, $16

In their cookbook, *Once upon a Tart,* owners Frank Mentesana and Jerome Audureau tell the story of their shop's phenomenal success as a prime savory and sweet tart destination. Their search for the perfect space led them to 135 Sullivan Street, a beat-up looking storefront that had in fact been a bakery a hundred years earlier. The cluttered basement revealed the original fixtures, glass pedestals, and shelving still intact. Once cleaned up and installed, these vintage touches are now an integral part of the quaint interior space with bright yellow walls, pressed tin ceilings, and not just tarts on display. Breakfast and lunch are served daily to a loyal clientele (one customer comes in every morning for two scones, one for him and one for his dog), but for the dessert connoisseur, the sweet tarts, freshly baked on premises with delicate butter crust, are the main attraction. The flavors change seasonally and the fruit tarts emphasize the freshness of whatever is ripe and best at the moment—plums, peaches, blueberries, pears. The chocolate pear tart we sampled was a lovely mélange of textures and flavors: delicate butter crust, rich chocolate cream, and ripe fruit. What more could you ask for?

## Greenmarket

Sixteen locations in Manhattan

Phone for locations, days, and hours: 212-477-3220

On a balmy spring, summer, fall, or, for the hardy, winter day, do what the chefs do: Go to the greenmarket.

Tourists to Europe come back to New York raving about the bowls of extraordinary fresh fruits so often brought to the table as dessert in sunny climates like Italy's and Spain's. It's an experience you can easily duplicate with freshly harvested, high-quality produce you buy directly from the folks who grew it in New York's neighboring rural areas: plump, juicy, tree- and vine-ripened strawberries, raspberries, plums, peaches, melons, and pears.

Sixteen greenmarkets are scattered around Manhattan alone, most open one or two days a week. The official starting time for most of them is 8 a.m. but if you want the pick of the crop, the earlier you get there, the better. Remember, you're competing with all those high-ranking chefs, each casting eagle eyes over what will become the seasonal specialties they take such pride in.

The largest and most famous greenmarket is the one at Union Square, open four days a week, where early-morning shopping is almost a blood sport. As at its citywide siblings, you can also find locally made cheeses, ciders, jams, and pastries. "No fat; no sugar" is the claim to greatness made by many of the bakers, with about the results you've come to recognize. A notch above are seasonal fruit pies with delicate crusts from Breezy Hill Orchards and, from Hawthorne Valley Farm, rich brownies and big chocolate chip and ginger cookies.

Beyond Union Square, we look for New Jersey

baker Tom Halick, whose Not Just Rugelach stand has rugelach we, and more rugelach-discerning friends, regard as among the best in the city. Weekends you can spot him at TriBeCa (Saturday) and 77th Street and Columbus Avenue (Sunday).

## osteria del circo

❋ *120 West 55th Street bet. Sixth and Seventh Avenues*
PHONE: 212-265-3636
CREDIT CARDS: AmEx, DC, MC, V
PRICE RANGE: $6–10; five tasting desserts, $12

For "Ladies and Gentlemen, Boys and Girls of All Ages," Osteria del Circo introduces itself on its website. That gives you some idea of the pleasure principle at work in this lighter-hearted sibling of Le Cirque 2000.

Both restaurants are the pampered creations of the ebullient Maccioni family, and I doubt there's a time when you won't find at least one of them on hand, ringmastering the proceedings.

The carnival tent atmosphere was designed by Adam Tihany: gold stars hanging from the ceiling, sculptured monkeys frolicking near the striped pole, a trapeze sailing over the bar.

Even the desserts come on festive hand-painted ceramic plates. And, yes, the desserts are festive, too, inspired versions of Maccioni family favorites: the famous *bomboloncini* (light Tuscan doughnuts) come filled with a variety of creams. Cannoli shells are stuffed with their chocolate-and-hazelnut-flecked ricotta cream just before being rushed to your table, so they're still crunchy. You can even indulge in the original crème brûlée Le Cirque, the standard by which all others have since been judged.

The Maccionis will smilingly lead you to a just-for-dessert table in the dining room if one is available. Call ahead, or just stop by and ask.

## le cirque 2000

✷ *455 Madison Avenue bet. 50th and 51st Streets*
PHONE: 212-303-7799
CREDIT CARDS: AmEx, DC, Disc, MC, V
PRICE RANGE: $10–13

For a real taste of culinary history (at a tab below three figures), betake yourself to the opulent bar of Le Cirque 2000 and have that legendary crème brûlée of Le Cirque on site. You'll be dining in one of the grandest rooms of the venerable Villard Houses. And the crème brûlée is the one with which Papa Maccioni first thrilled New Yorkers, a paper-thin crisp of browned sugar over a pool of ambrosian custard. It's just one of about eighteen choices, including a masterful fruit-based soufflé and a coconut mystère (served with coconut sorbet lollipops). It must be circus time again.

## otto

✷ *1 Fifth Avenue at 8th Street*
PHONE: 212-995-9559
CREDIT CARDS: AmEx, DC, MC, V
PRICE RANGE: $5–8

The designer pizzas and "little plates" have brought their own crowds to Otto, but for dessert cognoscenti the draw is definitely the gelato. How much art and craft can go into the making of gelato? Chef Meredith Kurtzman went to Italy to learn. And the knowledge she returned with—coupled with her own creative imagination—will have you shamelessly piling up the plates on your table.

Of course, you have to try the olive oil gelato (you'll taste a touch of sea salt), served with tart blood oranges in a wine syrup. It's a conversation-stopper, but don't mix and match it with the ever-changing fantasy of sweeter offerings. Most popular, with reason, is the goat cheese ricotta gelato, combined with wine-poached mission figs and candied walnuts. We loved a banana gelato, drizzled with chocolate sauce and dried cherries, and a vanilla gelato with tangerine sorbet and meringue.

A few flavors, including a not-to-be-ignored hazelnut stracciatella, grace the printed menu. But it's essential that you inquire about that day's gelato specials. You can get basic two- or three-gelato tasting plates, but those are just teases.

The narrow dark-wood room beyond the bar leads into a brighter, more open room looking out on Washington Mews, and regulars include art-smart locals, a number with toddlers and strollers during our midday visits. Everyone looks happy, knowing they can promenade away the pounds along the historic northern border of Washington Square with its row of elegant nineteenth-century Henry Jamesian houses.

## park avenue café

❊ *100 East 63rd Street bet. Park and
Lexington Avenues*
PHONE: 212-644-1900
CREDIT CARDS: AmEx, DC, Disc, MC, V
PRICE RANGE: desserts, $9–11; biscotti, $7

Award-winning pastry chef Richard Leach is an unassuming

man with a talent for the spectacular. The desserts he creates for Park Avenue Café arrive at your table as architectural stunners with cages and arches of spun and drawn sugar balancing on chocolate domes, or towers of mousse supporting cantilevered cookies. Chef Leach shrugs off such showmanship as all in a day's work—"It keeps me entertained," he says, noting that one of his concerns is whether the waiter will be able to carry it up the stairs. When the creation arrives the diner is hesitant to plunge in a fork while admiring the artistry. Just don't wait too long—your ice cream will start to melt, or your warm banana custard may cool off—because these are desserts as much to be savored as marveled at. Go ahead and crack the shell of the best-selling chocolate cube whose interior oozes with espresso mascarpone mousse and chocolate sorbet set on a meringue base decorated with honey-flavored chocolate tuiles. Enjoy the warm homey flavors of caramelized apples on walnut brioche that comes with sour cream ice cream and spiced pannacotta, and don't forget the candied walnuts, most important. In nearly every dessert Chef Leach includes a hot item, a cold item, and an item at room temperature to "interest and please customers."

While you're eating, feeling deeply self-indulgent, notice the charming, light-drenched, flower-filled surroundings—street-level windows face west on Park Avenue—and the Americana that decorates the walls behind the green-checked banquettes: here, a cookie jar collection; there, a collection of vintage rolling pins; and everywhere, whirligigs in the shape of Uncle Sam. Open for lunch and dinner, Park Avenue Café is pricey for a full meal but reasonable as, say, a late-afternoon dessert destination guaranteed to leave you feeling both impressed and relaxed. As a memento of your visit, buy a copy of Leach's gorgeous, full-color cookbook, *Sweet Seasons*, which illustrates many of these creations; he'll be happy to autograph it for you.

# payard patisserie & bistro

❄ *1032 Lexington bet. 73rd and 74th Streets*
PHONE: 212-717-5252
CREDIT CARDS: AmEx, MC, V
PRICES: most fancy pastries, $3.75–4.50;
bistro desserts, $7–9

On any given Saturday, Payard is packed and buzzing with stylish customers enjoying light snacks and pastries in the front patisserie, or multicourse lunches in the quieter, dark-paneled bistro dining room. (A tea menu is also offered from 3:30 to 5 p.m. Monday through Saturday.) It seems the perfect place to indulge oneself, after a morning of gallery going or shopping, with the best of French pastry and bistro fare. Owner (with Daniel Boulud) and patissier is Francois Payard while Philippe Bertineau presides over the bistro menu that offers its own composed desserts—upside-down bittersweet dark chocolate soufflé with pistachio ice cream, for example, or verbena and raspberry crème brûlée. An exclusively dessert-oriented visit will get you seated in the front room, after you've had a good look at the fancy pastries on display. If you find yourself wondering what's what, it's often instructive to eavesdrop on what's being ordered by the regulars. "Une religieuse!" demanded a woman in French on the day we visited. No, she was not asking for a priest, but for the coffee-flavored chocolate confection whose cocoa-colored exterior is said to resemble the homespun habits of French nuns. All the classic French pastries are here in Payard's particular and meticulous rendition, along with exquisite fruit tarts, napoleons (we sampled the impossibly delicate raspberry version), éclairs, entire cakes (the domed Le Louvre is a popular chocolate-hazelnut creation), and across the room, Payard's own chocolates. At holiday time, Payard sells cake-decorating kits for kids ($25), and for your wedding they'll create a gorgeous, multitiered cake that you'll spend the rest of your life living up to. Whatever your pleasure, it will assuredly be provided with that soupçon of elegance that makes true French style.

# podunk

❋ *231 East 5th Street bet. Second Avenue and Cooper Square*
PHONE: 212-677-7722
CASH ONLY
PRICE RANGE: cookies, $0.75; cupcakes, $1.50; cake slices, $2.75–3.75; teas for two, $22–30; children's tea, $8; birthday tea, $10 per participant; student tea for one, $8

Elspeth Treadwell's self-described tearoom/coffeehouse/ bakery is usually fragrant with the aroma of freshly baked cardamom cake, a Scandinavian specialty served with a choice of apricot-ginger or cayenne-lingonberry sauces. "We start from scratch and bake all day," she says. "People love the 'warm from the oven' aspect of what they come across each time they visit." Warm as well is Treadwell's friendly presence as she jogs between front counter and kitchen, whipping up everything from cupcakes and cookies to layer cakes, buttery scones, and savories. While you are welcome to order one or more of anything with tea, coffee, cappuccino, or espresso, Podunk also offers eight different tea menus that include both savories and sweets: smorgasbord, chocolate, rustic, nibbler, and cookie, as well as a children's milk-and-cupcake tea, which becomes a birthday tea with the addition of a birthday layer cake plus candles. Podunk is exceptionally kid-friendly—sitting on the floor is totally acceptable, for grownups too—and the atmosphere is of a country antiques shop, which in fact it is. All the furniture, Treadwell's passionately acquired collection of rustic country pieces, is for sale. "Regular customers get angry when their favorite chair is sold," she says. Pre-Podunk, Treadwell was an "office person, in cubicles all my life." With the opening of her charming little storefront tea room in 2002, she's realized a dream—that of pulling together everything she cares about: baking, antiques, and a country way of life. Podunk, she has said, is where she's from.

# poseidon bakery

❖ *629 9th Avenue bet. 44th and 45th Streets*
PHONE: 212-757-6173
CREDIT CARDS: MC, V
PRICE RANGE: pastries by the piece, $1.85–2.10;
cookies, $11.95/lb; strudel, $8.25/lb

Has the west side of Ninth Avenue been designated a landmark area? It gets our vote. In a few blocks in the 40s you can still find old-fashioned, no-frill purveyors of some of the freshest fish and greatest cheeses in New York and, at Poseidon Bakery, the finest Greek pastries, bar none.

Phyllo dough is the one essential in the best-known of the Greek pastries, and Poseidon is the last pastry shop in the city that makes its own, fresh, every day—light, flaky, tender. In Poseidon's baklava, it folds around beautifully balanced layers of walnuts and almonds, drenched in a cinnamon-spiced honey-based syrup. In Trigana, it surrounds an almond paste triangle. Kombehaye is a light fluffy sponge cake wrapped in phyllo.

Look around, and pick what appeals to you. Everything is described; and if one of the third- or fourth-generation family members is at the counter—Tony, Lily, or their son Paul—they'll go into enthusiastic detail. We loved the Galactoburiko, a rich custard pastry, and Kourambiedes, butter almond cookies in a snowfall of powdered sugar. The mixed-nut brittle is sensational.

Don't be surprised at the unassuming atmosphere. This is a mom-and-pop (and -son) operation; they put their time and money into first-rate ingredients and TLC, as they have for decades.

---

## quintessence

✳ *566 Amsterdam Avenue bet. 87th and 88th Streets*
PHONE: 212-501-9700

✳ *353 East 78th Street bet. First and*
*Second Avenues*
PHONE: 212-734-0888

✳ *263 East 10th Street bet. First Avenue and*
*Avenue A*
PHONE: 646-654-1804

CREDIT CARDS: AmEx, MC, V

PRICE RANGE: average entrees, $10.50–14; desserts, $7

How about a trip to the cutting edge? For foodies, "raw" is where it's at, and Quintessence is the best place we've found to get a taste. At Quintessence nothing is cooked or baked—from appetizers to desserts—and the results are a revelation. Quintessence is part of the now widespread raw-food movement that first gained national prominence with the opening of the five-star Roxanne's restaurant in Larkspur, California, in 2002. Raw-food cooks disdain stoves or ovens using instead dehydrators, food processors, and blenders. Cooking, say raw-food enthusiasts, not only destroys valuable enzymes in food but also depletes it of important vitamins and minerals. Raw foods, they believe, reverse the aging process and enhance youth, beauty, and vitality. Naturally, it has many celebrity adherents.

We went to Quintessence—with its coolly relaxing minimalist interior—to experience an entire raw meal, with a special anticipation of desserts that friends had recommended. The desserts are mainly pies with crusts made from a dense, ground, tasty mixture of soaked almonds, soaked walnuts and apricots with other flavoring. Coconut pie's carob-nut crust is filled with young, creamy "live" coconut. It was exceptionally light and subtle, and though interesting, we preferred the more intense pecan pie made with raw pecans and fresh dates—the surprisingly predominant flavor. We also sampled a fine mango-peach pie with organic chocolate topping and a deliciously fresh fruit plate. The three-layer mud slide pie featuring layers of pecan fudge carob mousse and mesquite cream in an almond-walnut crust is understandably one of the most popular desserts on the menu.

## rice to riches

&#10023; *37 Spring Street bet. Lafayette and Elizabeth Streets*
PHONE: 212-274-0008
CREDIT CARDS: AmEx, MC, V
PRICE RANGE: 8-ounce "solo" portion, $4.50; sumo (serves four), $12.50

It could be the cafeteria on the starship Enterprise: a rice-grain-shaped stark white interior with glowing orange Lucite accents, photographic murals of fruit, and a long curving counter fitted out with big bowls of just one dessert: rice pudding! But not exactly grandma's version. Here, pastry chef Jemal Edwards, formerly of Montrachet and Nobu, has created eighteen unusual and exotic variations on this comfort-food favorite. We loved the surprising elegance of Bottomless Pear (with anise) and the tropical blast of Surrender to Mango (with lime). Coffee Collapse (yes, all the names are jokey) has a lovely cardamom top note, Chocolate Cherry Crime Scene tastes like a cherry cordial, and Pistachio Protest (with sage) is smooth and subtle, but the sage did not assert itself. If you're crying, "Where is grandma's pudding?" it's here too—look no further than Understanding Vanilla (with Indonesian vanilla) and Cinnamon Sling (replete with reassuring brown sugar and dark raisins). Puddings are served cold but can be warmed on request and there are three crunchy toppings: Pandam Rice Flake flavored with lemongrass powder, cardamom and ginger; Spirit, an oat and coconut crumble; and Mischief, whose ingredients are "secret." You can eat at one of three tiny round plastic tables suspended from ceiling poles, but most of the business here is brightly packaged takeout. Look for the weekly specials and for Rice to Riches openings in other neighborhoods, as an expansion is planned.

~~~~~~~~~~~~~~~~~~~~~~~~~~~~~~~~~~~~~~~~~~~~

# ristorante bussola—gelateria

❊ *65 Fourth Avenue bet. 9th and 10th Streets*
PHONE: 212-254-1940
CREDIT CARDS: AmEx, MC, V
PRICE RANGE: cups, depending on the flavor, $3–6;
pint, $7–9

Sicilian-born Gino Cammarata has been making small-batch artisanal gelato since he was a kid in Sortino, a small town near Siracusa. Chef for twenty years at the adjoining Ristorante Bussola, he makes a limited number of superb gelato and sorbet flavors using top-quality Sicilian fruits and flavorings. He uses Sicilian stone-ground pistachios to create the classic "green gold" flavor that leaves your tongue believing it's tasting the fresh nuts. Hazelnut, for which he is famous, is thrillingly intense; and his tangerine (*mandarina*) sorbet is, we think, the best citrus flavor in the city, if you really like tart. Bussola's powerful espresso gelato seems to have been made just seconds before it melts in your mouth. He urged us to try it Sicilian-style, spread on a salty, olive-oiled crostini—a revelation!—and suggested we eat his creamy, luscious ricotta gelato dribbled with best-quality balsamico. It's a sweet-and-sour phenomenon that rocks your taste buds. Cammarata recently introduced his brioche con gelato, the sweetest, fattest ice cream sandwich this side of Palermo, and will fill cannoli shells with gelato if you wish. Like many other food establishments in New York, Ristorante Bussola suffered in the wake of September 11. Let's hope Cammarata's authentic haute Sicilian food and especially those great gelati will be around to see us through the hard times ahead.

## ruby et violette's gourmet cookie company

❈ *457 West 50th Street bet. Ninth and Tenth Avenues*
PHONE: 212-582-6720
www.rubyetviolette.com
CREDIT CARDS: AmEx, MC, V
PRICE RANGE: single cookie, $1.25; dozen, $15

With every corner store and gourmet market offering some disc dubbed chocolate chip, chocolate chunk, or Toll House, choosing the best of these cookies may seem foolhardy. But we've yet to see a list that doesn't put Ruby et Violette's at, or close to, the top.

You may be familiar with the story of how Wendy Gayner shut down her thriving Sag Harbor cookie business after her daughter suffered a traumatic car accident, then reopened in Manhattan a couple of years ago. The happy ending is that the daughter recovered—and New Yorkers can once again indulge themselves on these brown-sugary, chewy master-pieces, loaded with chunks of semi-sweet chocolate.

With no other additions, those are indeed "Perfect," a name with which we agree. But then there are those other forty-two varieties you'll want to try, with everything from infu-sions of espresso, dulce de leche, crème de menthe, and coffee Cognac to added bits of dried cherries, crystallized ginger, roasted chestnuts, and pistachios mixed in along with the chocolate.

You can pick out your own at their pretty boutique in, of all places, Hell's Kitchen. With a hefty cookie going for just $1.25 (or $15 for a baker's dozen), you can be generous with yourself. The very experience is a choco-sybarite's delight. If you order two dozen or more, Ruby et Violette will ship or deliver.

Oh, they also do chocolate-chipped "Moon Pies," "Oreos," "Twinkies," and other childhood delights. For the kids, you know.

## sarabeth's

*new york's 50+ best places to enjoy dessert*

❊ *Hotel Wales, 1295 Madison Avenue bet. 92nd and 93rd Streets*
PHONE: 212-410-7335

❊ *Whitney Museum of American Art, 945 Madison Avenue at 75th Street*
PHONE: 212-570-3670

❊ *423 Amsterdam Avenue bet. 80th and 81st Streets*
PHONE: 212-496-6280

❊ *Chelsea Market (see listing)*
CREDIT CARDS: AmEx, MC, V

Our favorite Sarabeth location is the Whitney because, frankly, it has the best art-celebrity watching—especially weekdays. You can depend on Sarabeth's baked goods and know you'll be getting a nice piece of chocolate mousse cake or a good vanilla bread pudding, strawberry shortcake, or Ciao Bella gelato with your coffee or tea, but you might also get a look at regulars like Yoko Ono or Chuck Close, who have been known to stop by. We also like the echo-y hum of the building that fills the air above our heads as we contemplate a show we might have just seen, or plan to see (you don't have to pay museum entry to go to Sarabeth's one flight down). You feel your dessert is a proper reward for having caught some culture and shocked a few brain cells out of torpor, even if you went no further than Calder's Circus, on permanent view in the lobby. NOTE: The museum is closed on Monday. Tues.–Fri. 11a.m.–3:45 p.m.; Sat.–Sun. 10 a.m.–4:30 p.m.

# seppi's

❋ *127 West 58th Street bet. Sixth and*
  *Seventh Avenues*
PHONE: 212-708-7444
CREDIT CARDS: AmEx, Disc, MC, V
PRICE RANGE: $7–10; Sunday chocolate brunch, $24

This is the kind of place you love to happen upon by accident, then sit in its cozy confines, congratulating yourself on your good fortune. That's just what we did on a rainy afternoon, stopping to chat with chef-owner Claude Alain Sulliard, who was lunching late at the bar.

Newspapers at the door, mismatched old posters and prints adorning the pressed tin walls, blackboards with the specials and wines of the day, long hours (11:30 a.m. to 2 a.m.); all reflect the smiling Claude's commitment to establishing a haven where you can drop by, "be comfortable," linger, and order as little (or as much) as you choose. For desserts, that means much what you'd find at that little place you'd love to happen upon in Paris: tarte tatin, crème brûlée à la noisette, gratin de poires, soufflé au chocolat blanc et amantes, even an assortment de chocolats Jacques Torres— our favorite among all the city's chocolates, and, here, without the excursion to Brooklyn.

This particular gem lies just around the block behind Carnegie Hall. If you're planning a visit before a Sunday matinee, it might be best not to attempt a last-minute run for your seats. The special prix fixe Sunday brunch is "Inspired by Chocolate," and includes such temptations as a chocolate mimosa, phyllo-wrapped eggs on smoked salmon with cocoa brioche, and, for closure, an extravagant chocolate buffet.

# norma's at the parker meridien

❉ *118 West 57th Street bet. Sixth and Seventh Avenues*

PHONE: 212-708-7460

CREDIT CARDS: AmEx, DC, Disc, MC, V

PRICE RANGE: $6–15

If you're an earlier bird than Seppi's 11:30 a.m. opening, the Parker Meridien, which shelters Seppi's, offers breakfast and brunch fare at Norma's that should jolt the sweetest tooth. Among the more fanciful temptations served in this sleekly modernist room: chocolate decadence french toast, the rich brioche slices cloaked in strawberries, pistachios, and chocolate sauce; mango papaya brown butter cinnamon crèpes; caramelized chocolate banana waffle napoleon; raspberry risotto oatmeal; and Waz-Za, a waffle with fruit inside and out with a crunchy brûlée top. Norma's closes at 3 p.m.

# serendipity 3

❉ *225 East 60th Street bet. Second and Third Avenues*

PHONE: 212-838-3531

www.serendipity3.com

CREDIT CARDS: AmEx, DC, Disc, MC, V

PRICE RANGE: "Frrrozen" hot chocolate, $6.95; desserts, $7–20 (banana split)

A chocoholic checkpoint for fifty years, Serendipity 3 serves up its famous "Frrrozen" hot chocolate in a warm, funky ambience that has charmed New Yorkers—celebrities and otherwise—since 1954. Served up in a mega-goblet with a pile of whipped cream and two straws, the slushy drink blends twelve kinds of super-delicious chocolate with cocoa powders, milk, sugar, and ice. The restaurant/gift shop also sells it in three different forms: as a packaged mix (just add milk, ice, and blend) that you can take home to maintain your chocolate high; as a mocha-colored lip gloss that smells great but is unflavored; and as bath and body gel (just don't squirt it on ice cream).

Serendipity 3's cachet among the sundae-seeking glitterati seems never to have lessened since Andy Warhol declared it his favorite sweet shop and Jackie Kennedy brought Caroline and John-John in for the famous foot-long hot dogs. The funky, ice cream parlor ambience, complete with Tiffany-style lampshades, continues to charm hordes of New Yorkers who go not just for the humongous drug store sundaes, banana splits, or lemon ice box pie but also for hamburgers and vegetarian chili. There's a children's menu (as well as toys and other things for kids and grownups to buy on the way out) and a general atmosphere of fun being had by all. You're just not a New Yorker until you've been to Serendipity 3.

## Favorite Dessert Destinations for Kids (of All Ages)

Ice cream, candy, nice gooey cupcakes—served up in a relaxed atmosphere—is usually all that's required to provide youngsters and their folks with a special and pleasurable sweet-centered experience. But sometimes frenzy is in order, and that, along with gummy-bear overload, is what you get at **Dylan's Candy Bar** (1011 Third Ave. at 60th St., 646-735-0078) just half a block from Serendipity 3. With 5,000 types of candy, sold by the pound, arranged in museum-like displays (note the gummi-embedded staircase) and an ice cream and frozen yogurt bar and soda fountain downstairs, you'll have a hard time prying your kids from this sugary nirvana (available for parties). For real food in a Brooklyn-themed setting with baseball and subway motifs, **Brooklyn Diner** (212 West 57th St. bet. Seventh Ave. and Broadway, 212-977-1957) offers burgers, a fifteen-bite Brooklyn hot dog, and sandwiches to be topped off with a big-enough-for-two Valrhona chocolate fudge sundae, lemon meringue pie with meringue *that* high, plus strawberry-topped cheesecake. At **Mars 2112** (1633 Broadway at 51st St., 212-582-2112), a made-for-kids simulated trip to the Red Planet can lead to an Earthling-friendly meal of chicken fingers capped with a three-scoop Polar Ice Caps sundae or andromeda apple pie all served in a subterranean Martian dining room. Older kids and teens will dig the rock-and-roll ambience—Cadillacs and guitars—of the **The Hard Rock Cafe** (221 West 57th St. bet. Seventh Ave. and Broadway, 212-489-6565), where the dessert menu offers a dozen selections including chocolate-chip cookie pie or a brownie sundae served in a huge margarita glass, down-home apple cobbler, and a four-layer chocolate cake. The "Lil' Rocker" menu features a hot fudge sundae for $1.99. Further uptown, **DTUT** (1626 Second Ave. bet. 84th and 85th Sts., 212-327-1327), a funky coffeehouse furnished à la thrift shop, has piles of kid-pleasing desserts, including a DIY S'mores for Two served with its own table-top cooker. In the Village, the Tex-Mex **Cowgirl Hall of Fame** (519 Hudson St. at 10th St., 212-633-1133) delights kids with its Western mini museum, displays of barbed wire, and funky gift shop selling water-squirting pistols, beaded belts, and such. The dessert menu features their famous "ice cream baked potato" in which the vegetable is simulated with a cocoa-dusted, potato-shaped chunk of ice cream, whipped cream stands in for sour cream, green-dyed chopped pecans make like chives, and banana buttercream is shaped like a butter pat. Careful: Your kid might think he's getting a real potato for dessert and burst into tears! There are pies and cobblers too. While the ice cream-drenched Belgian waffles and the "little bee" cartoon motifs at **Petite Abeille** (400 West 14th St. at 9th Ave. and several other locations; 212-727-1505) never fail to enchant children, the regular dining menu, with its Belgian specialties and forty-five types of Belgian beers, makes this a perfect parent-child destination for brunch, lunch, or dinner.

Ice cream shops not to be missed include the venerable **Chinatown Ice Cream Factory** (65 Bayard St. bet. Elizabeth and Mott Sts., 212-608-4170) with its weird and wonderful flavors and bright yellow dragon T-shirt always available in kid sizes, and **Brooklyn Ice Cream Factory** (1 Old Fulton St. at Water St., Dumbo, Brooklyn; 718-246-3963), located in a former fireboat house in a little park with a view of Manhattan. See also listings in this book for **@SQC**, **Elephant and Castle**, **Columbus Bakery**, **Edgar's Café**, **Good Enough to Eat**, **Magnolia Bakery**, **Cupcake Café**, **Podunk**, **Sarabeth's**, and **Yura**.

# strip house

✻ *13 East 12th Street bet. Fifth Avenue and University Place*
PHONE: 212-328-0000
CREDIT CARDS: AmEx, DC, MC, V
PRICE RANGE: $8–12

new york's 50+ best places to enjoy dessert

Go for the chocolate cake. We're not the first ones to say it, nor the last, as long as chef René Luger remains in charge. This is not a molten chocolate cake, chocolate mousse cake, chocolate decadence, or gateau au chocolat. It's the chocolate layer cake that is the emotional equivalent for many Americans of Proust's madeleine, with alternating layers of chocolate sponge cake and thick, dark chocolate custard under an even richer chocolate frosting. In this case, twenty-four thin layers stand so tall and moist that each slice trembles when you touch it with your fork.

Strip House occupies the site where Asti's waiters once burst into song at the drop of an ice cube. The Italian songsters are gone, but Strip House pays homage to their memory with dense hangings of Asti's photos of mostly bygone celebrities against the red-flocked wallpaper. There are also some vintage photos of flirtatious bare-bosomed belles of the 1920s, giving the darkly lit room a raffish look.

For dessert alone, you'll probably be seated up-front in the bar and lounge. And, of course, you can choose among René Luger's other specialties, like the eye-opening Clou du Mont coffee crème brûlée, served with a pot of Clou du Mont Vintage 2002 coffee. Or a warm crêpe soufflé with vanilla ice cream melting inside it, drenched with mandarin oranges and blackberries.

Go for the chocolate cake.

## The Chocolate Show—Don't miss it!

November in New York means chocolate—three whole days devoted to celebrating the world's most popular confection with tastings, culinary demonstrations, and even a chocolate fashion show! Don't miss this fabulous annual event where fifty top chocolate makers and producers of chocolate-related products assemble to meet the public and showcase their wares. Renowned chefs and chocolatiers will be on hand to demonstrate their art; there'll be book signings, educational exhibits, and children's activities too. The place: The Metropolitan Pavilion, 125 West 18th St., bet. Sixth and Seventh Aves. For tickets: 212-889-5112 (local); 866-CHO-CNYC (national) or online at www.chocolateshow.com (for dates, as well). Tickets: adults, $15; seniors (65+) and students (I.D. required), $12; children 6–14, $6; children under six, free.

## sullivan street bakery

* 73 Sullivan Street bet. Broome and
  Spring Streets
  PHONE: 212-334-9435
* 533 West 47th Street bet. Tenth and
  Eleventh Avenues
  PHONE: 212-265-5580
  CASH ONLY
  PRICE RANGE: slices and individual servings, $1.50–2.50;
  whole cakes, $20

James Lahey's celebrated bakery provides the highest quality bread to more than 200 restaurants and specialty stores throughout the city, but you have to travel to the glass-fronted Sullivan Street store—with two sunny benches out front—for his marvelously authentic dolci baked fresh daily from recipes learned and researched in Italy. These are not the usual creamy confections found at pasticcerias around town; Lahey's crostatas and tortas are what you'd be more likely to find in an Italian home in Tuscany, exactly where he found the recipes. Among the delectable crostatas are two classics: Crostata de Marmellata, with a tender crust—something like shortbread—flavored with almonds, orange, and honey and filled with raspberry or apricot preserves; and Crostata di Ricotta whose rum-tinged cheese filling is flecked with chocolate and candied orange peel. The Tortino de Cioccolato, with its soft crunch and delicate melting texture, is a small individual cake to savor at any time of day. Lahey also offers biscotti (including biscotti crumbs for sprinkling on ice cream); airy, crunchy cookies with the unusual name Ossi de Morti because they actually resemble bones; and seasonal dolci (panettone, pumpkin, and squash crostatas, and tarte tatin). We can't help mentioning that this is also a destination for wonderfully tasty, very thin-crusted, rectangular pizzas topped with savory vegetable toppings—irresistible snacks that could easily fuel your walk home carrying this bakery's marvelous breads and take-away desserts.

~~~~~~~~~~~~~~~~~~~~~~~~~~~~~~~~~~~~~~~~~~~~~~~~~~~~~~~~

## sweet-n-tart café

❉ *20 Mott Street bet. Park Row and Pell Street*
PHONE: 212-964-0380
CREDIT CARDS: AmEx, MC, V
PRICE RANGE: sweets (several per order), about $3.75;
tong shui, $2.25–3.75

Want to take a quantum leap from your basic fortune cookie? The place most highly recommended by our Chinese-American friends is Sweet-n-Tart Café. A Cantonese restaurant known for its outstanding dim-sum, Sweet-n-Tart also boasts a unique and substantial dessert menu featuring *tong shui*, healing soups—usually served as a comfort food in Chinese homes—whose ingredients, in combination, are said to address specific health issues. The Chinese believe that Double Boiled Papaya with Snow Fungus & Almond (actually sweet & bitter apricot seeds), the one we sampled, has the power to cure coughs, fortify the immune system, regulate stomach ("Qi") energy, soothe the liver, and more. While drinking this soup sweetened with rock sugar and flecked with almonds and red papaya chunks, it's nice to be assured that the snow fungus cleanses the lungs. Generally speaking, says owner Spencer Chan, *tong shui* (a Cantonese delicacy) are eaten after a rich meal to restore the body's yin-yang balance, but also as an afternoon snack. Soups aside, Sweet-n-Tart also features sweets—also with healing properties—that you can easily eat with fingers or chopsticks. We particularly liked the deep-fried, banana-stuffed sesame balls, and a creamy, ginger-milk pudding with a surprise of red bean paste to be spooned up from the bottom. While these desserts may strike the Western palate as unusual—a far cry from the expected scoop of ice cream or fortune cookie—they are a pleasing introduction to an aspect of Chinese, specifically Cantonese, cuisine that we rarely experience and know little of. Enjoy Sweet-n-Tart dim sum and desserts in the pleasant upstairs dining room, if you can, where a party of six or more rates a private room.

Sweet-n-Tart Café on the north end of Mott Street (No. 76) serves those now-ubiquitous, slightly chewable fresh fruit tapioca shakes that kids love, along with dumplings, soups, and lo mein.

# teany

�֍ *90 Rivington Street bet. Ludlow and*
   *Orchard Streets*

PHONE: 212-475-9190

CREDIT CARDS: AmEx, MC, V

PRICE RANGE: cake slices, $4–6; Tea for One, $14,
for Two, $25

Vegan rock star Moby owns light, bright, and 100-percent vegetarian Teany (pronounced "teeny"), a cozy tearoom with a
sidewalk cafe and about nine round aluminum tables for two
inside. Yes, there are savories—generously portioned salads,
sandwiches, crostini, and such—but sweet-craving vegetarians
and vegans, and omnivores, too come here expressly for the
large selection of dairy-free and egg-free desserts. At least nine
kinds of cakes, of which six are vegan, include the deservedly
popular chocolate peanut butter bombe (a candy bar gone to
heaven), a finely textured soy-based faux cheesecake with fresh
fruit, and a meltingly light strawberry shortcake, made of fresh
vanilla-flavored cake layers frosted with dairy-free pastry cream
that even buttercream-craving tastebuds could love. Cakes are
shipped in from Vegan Treats (www.vegantreats.com), a small
Pennsylvania bakery, where Danielle Konya wields the wisk. A
generous slab of her fallen chocolate soufflé cake, or iced carrot cake, or strawberry-rhubarb pie should satisfy any major
craving. For minor cravings, Teany's chef Amanda Cohen makes
delicious vegan petit-fours, brownies, and cookies. They can be
ordered separately or as part of the delightful Tea for One and
Tea for Two, each of which also include savory tea sandwiches
and a scone with clotted cream and jam. A late-night romantic
special ($22), served between 9 p.m. and midnight, offers a
choice of any two cocktails and any two cakes (chocolate
strongly advised as being "most romantic"). A good selection
of teas are sold by the pot.

# terrance brennan's seafood & chop house

❋ *565 Lexington Avenue at 50th Street*

PHONE: 212-838-5665

CREDIT CARDS: AmEx, MC, V

PRICE RANGE: $12

The corner of Lexington Avenue and 50th Street would never be mistaken for the French Quarter. But in designing his Seafood & Chop House, chef Terrance Brennan has done—but not overdone—a masterful job of making you feel you've entered an elegant, quietly casual corner of the Old World. The bar-lounge area to the right, where you'll probably be accommodated, has long-fringed lamp shades, lots of deep red, and slatted wooden blinds to mask the workaday world outside.

Inside, Terrance Brennan is bringing back one of the luxe-est desserts from the glory days of haute cuisine, crepes suzettes, prepared tableside with all the flourishes and pyrotechnics. Ask for a running commentary on what's going into the tangerine sauce pan before the flambé finale; it's part of the fun.

At Brennan's House they also flambé the baked Alaska tableside, adding a tart citrus-and-spice soup as a counterpoint to the caramelized meringue.

If you're not into Golden Age theatrics, there are such enticing alternatives as an almost pudding-moist flourless chocolate cake in a pool of delicate hazelnut sauce.

But go for the fireworks.

## Drinks with Your Dessert?

Choosing the perfect dessert wines, ports, Madeiras, and cognacs is another art, and another book, entirely. It can also double or triple the cost of a dessert outing in the blink of an eye. But...if you're feeling flush and celebratory, taking a first step into this special world of the oenophile can awaken a palate to a new sensation. The surest bet for novices is to throw yourself on the mercy of a good sommelier—as we did at Terrance Brennan's, where Wine Director Richard Shipman guided us through choices ranging from a refreshing Brachetto d'Acqui Ca Dio Mandorli (at $8 a flute) to accompany the baked Alaska to a spectacularly deep and fruity Ruster Ausbruch Feiler-Artinger 1998 ($22) with the crepes.

Like others of his peers, Richard Shipman prepares his list with specific pairings of wines and desserts in mind, even searching out an uncommon new wine for a specialty like the Crepes Suzettes.

Most restaurants offer their dessert wines by the glass. Look over the list, decide what your price limit is, and say so. A good wine steward is happy to know, and even happier to find someone who's honest and interested.

## toraya

❊ *17 East 71st Street bet. Madison and Fifth Avenues*
PHONE: 212-861-1700
CREDIT CARDS: AmEx, DC, MC, V
PRICE RANGE: wagashi, $3–4; desserts, $3–9

We visited this peaceful, skylit Japanese tearoom on a spring afternoon hoping to learn something about *wagashi*, the seasonal sweets that have been a part of this refined culture for centuries. Toraya—the oldest confectioner in Japan—dates to the sixteenth century when it began to serve the Imperial court. Only in 1980 did it open its first overseas shop in Paris and, in 1993, this little haven off Madison Avenue. Despite the company's ancient lineage, this branch of Toraya has a relaxed, modern feel. The waitresses wear jeans and white cotton blouses—not a kimono in sight—and all kinds of people come here knowing they'll be able to have a nice talk over a light lunch, or simply tea (the selection is marvelous) and *wagashi* or other desserts.

As you enter, displays of *wagashi* give you some idea of what to expect: exquisitely formed confections made of adzuki bean paste like nothing Westerners are used to. They are also pictured and explained on the menu, which devotes several pages to desserts, of which *wagashi* are just one category. We ordered a pot of roasted green tea, which is actually a golden color, and *uji no sato*, an amazing looking *wagashi* first introduced in 1802. It arrives—a bright, fuzzy green ball about an inch and a half in diameter sitting on a gray ceramic plate. The brilliant color is from a coating of *matcha* powder (powdered green tea) that adheres to a sticky rice flour skin, which in turn encloses a smooth red bean paste center. Cutting into the ball is almost traumatic: the lovely green powder falls away and the symmetry is destroyed. Could this be a Zen teaching on impermanence? Now you begin to understand the appeal of *wagashi*. While this is nothing like dessert-as-you-know-it, it's definitely an aesthetic experience worth having.

All around, people were ordering interesting looking things. A Japanese woman across the room was served a glass goblet of multicolored gelatin cubes, which she doused with brown sugar syrup and devoured ("very low calorie," the manager explained). A man was spooning up a large bowl of ice cream over shaved ice sprinkled with *matcha* powder ("Refreshing on a hot summer day. Not too sweet," he said). And two high school boys far off the pizza route came in with slung backpacks and ordered, amazingly, several *wagashi* each. What are they thinking, we wondered, as we watched them tuck into *zangetsu*, a soft ginger-flavored pancake shaped like the waning moon, and *fuji no tana*, a purple, white, and green layered block of bean jelly that celebrates the color of the wisteria blossom. We were thinking: You're not in Kansas anymore, kids.

### A "Museum" of Japanese Sweets

Entering the street-level doors of **Minamoto Kitchoan** (608 Fifth Ave. at 4th St.; 212-489-3747; www.kitchoan.com) is like going into a Zen retreat, so serene, so quiet. Nothing distracts from the ravishing still-life-like displays of *wagashi*, traditional Japanese confections so artfully wrapped and meticulously arranged that it's love at first sight.

In the Japanese tradition, sight is only one of the five senses that a dessert should satisfy. (The one you might not guess: sound, when you hear the names of individual pastries, like *shobumochi*, walnut-filled rice cake coated with green powder and exquisitely wrapped to look like a purple Japanese iris, or *momoaya*, shining white peaches suspended in a transparent jelly.)

Of all the world's desserts, Japan's are among the most refined and exotic. Getting to know them is a unique culinary adventure; making a selection among the many variations of the four basic types—jelly, sugar, rice cake, and baked—at Minamoto Kitchoan is an enchanting way to begin.

Each offering on display has its own descriptive note, and there is a handsome little brochure to guide you further. As you browse, imagine having a little tasting party of *wagashi* for your more sophisticated friends.

Oh, by the way, *kitchoan* means "house of happiness."

PRICE RANGE: mochi (rice cakes), $1–$2.50; wagashi, $1–13

# a glossary of dessert terms

Whether reading a menu or making a choice at a fancy pastry shop or down-home bakery, you're bound to encounter some of the following words and terms.

**apfelstrudel**: apple strudel; see *strudel*.

**assiette**: the French word for "plate"; an assortment of foods of a particular type arranged on a plate, as in "lemon assiette" describing a dessert of several lemon-flavored items.

**baba**: usually a small individual yeast-risen cake flavored with rum after baking.

**baked alaska**: a hot-and-cold dessert in which ice cream is surrounded by hot meringue on a base of liqueur-soaked sponge cake.

**bavarese**: Italian for Bavarian cream; see Bavarois.

**bavarian cream**: see Bavarois.

**bavarois** (bav-ar-WA): French term for a cold egg custard dessert mixed with whipped cream and flavored and set in a mold.

**belle-helene**: a cold dessert of poached pears served with vanilla ice cream and hot chocolate sauce.

**biscotti**: in Italian the word means "baked twice" and describes the way in which these crisp, nutty cookies are made in dozens of varieties; delicious with coffee or dunked in sweet wine.

**buche de noel**: a rolled Christmas cake filled and spread with chocolate or mocha buttercream that is made to look like a log and decorated with meringue mushrooms.

**gateau** (ga-TOH): the French word for "cake."

**cannoli**: the plural of cannolo ("cannon") a pastry tube filled with ricotta cream; the classic Sicilian dessert.

**caramel**: the deep golden-brown syrup that results when sugar is cooked and caramelized.

**cassata:** a rich Sicilian cake, usually sponge cake, filled with ricotta cream (like cannoli cream), covered with white sugar icing or marzipan and decorated with candied fruit.

**chantilly** (SHAHN-tee-ee): sweetened whipped cream; also *crème Chantilly.*

**charlotte**: a dessert made in a mold lined with ladyfingers, filled with fruit or other flavored custard, or mousse, or bavarois, and served unmolded.

**choux pastry**: a pastry used for making éclairs and cream-puffs that puffs out during baking and is then filled with cream or custard; also *pâte à choux.*

**clafoutis** (kla-FOO-tee): a French-style cake made by placing fruit (traditionally cherries) in a buttered dish, pouring in a pancake-like batter, and baking it; often served warm.

**chiboust**: a type of custard pastry cream, usually vanilla-flavored, that is blended while warm with stiffly beaten egg whites.

**crème brûlée**: a chilled cream-based custard dessert topped with a layer of usually brown sugar which is caramelized into a sweet brittle crust before serving.

**crepe**: a thin pancake made in a frying, or crepe, pan. Sweet crepes are often made with vanilla-flavored sugar, filled with creams or custard and served with powdered sugar. The famous crepe suzette is flavored with orange or tangerine and Grand Marnier or Curacao liqueur and served *en flambé* tableside.

**croquembouche**: usually a fancy, towering presentation composed of piled creampuffs stuck together with a caramel glaze; popular as a wedding cake.

**crostata**: a flat, shortbread type of Italian pastry, filled with fruit puree, usually raspberry or apricot.

**dacquoise**: a cake made from layers of hazelnut-flavored meringues filled with whipped cream.

**éclair**: finger- or log-shaped pastry filled with cream and glazed.

**financier** (fee-NAHN-cee-ay): a small, rectangular almond-flavored sponge cake, supposedly resembling a gold brick, hence the name.

**flan**: a caramelized egg custard.

**fraisier** (FRAY-zee-ay): a fancy cake made with fresh strawberries and strawberry jam.

**frangipane** (FRAN-zhuh-pan): almond cream.

**galette**: a flat, round cake, savory or sweet; sometimes a type of French tart.

**ganache** (gan-ASCH): a mixture of bittersweet chocolate and cream used as icing or filling in a cake or pastry.

**gianduja** (zhan-DU-ya): chocolate flavored with hazelnuts or almonds.

**key lime**: a variety of lime that is smaller, and more mild, than the common Persian lime, and more yellow than green.

**kouing-aman**: a large flat Breton cake made of buttery, cream-enriched bread dough and topped with caramelized sugar.

**kugelhopf**: an Austrian yeast cake baked in a crown-like mold and filled with raisins, currants, and sometimes fruit and nuts.

**kulfi**: a type of dense Indian ice cream made with a cream reduction.

**linzertorte**: an Austrian shortbread pastry flavored with ground almonds and grated lemon rind and topped with raspberry jam; named for the town of Linz, Austria.

**macaroon**: a round cookie, crunchy outside and soft inside, made with ground almonds, or almond paste, sugar, and egg whites; coconut macaroons substitute coconut for almonds.

**madeleine**: a small sponge cake, made in a seashell-shaped mold, usually flavored with lemon or orange; made famous by Marcel Proust in *Remembrance of Things Past,* in which the taste of the cake evoked memories.

**megeve** (meh-ZHEV): a cake made of crunchy white vanilla meringue, chocolate mousse, and ganache, topped with chocolate glaze; a Fauchon best-seller for eighty years.

**meringue**: egg whites stiffly beaten with sugar.

**meyer lemon**: a variety of lemon whose juice is considerably sweeter than that of regular lemons.

**mille-feuille** (mee-FOY): a napoleon; a small rectangular pastry made of multiple layers of puff pastry filled with cream mousseline (a pastry cream with 20 percent Chantilly whipped cream) and iced with royal icing or fondant.

**mont blanc** (Monte Bianco, Italian): named for the alpine peak that stands between France and Italy, a pastry claimed by both countries; composed of a mound of sweetened, vanilla-flavored chestnut puree that is "snow-capped" with whipped cream or Chantilly cream; often prepared on a tart-crust base. The Italian version is further flavored with brandy or Cognac; the Fauchon version is made in an almond tart shell filled with vanilla meringue, Chantilly cream, wild rose petal puree, and topped with piped chestnut cream.

**mousse**: a light, fluffy, cream-based mixture flavored with fruit puree or chocolate.

**napoleon**: see *Mille-feuille*.

**opera**: a rich French pastry composed of thin, alternating layers of almond sponge cake, mocha coffee cream, and dark chocolate ganache, topped with dark chocolate glaze and often decorated with edible gold leaf.

**panettone**: a sweet Italian Christmas cake made from a rich yeast dough containing raisins and candied fruit.

**pannacotta**: Italian for "cooked cream"; a heated, eggless cream made in a mold, much lighter than baked custard.

**paris-brest** (pa-ree-BREST): a wheel-shaped éclair filled with praline-flavored cream and sprinkled with almonds, created in 1891 to commemorate the famous Paris-Brest bicycle race. *Paris-Nice* is a variation without almonds.

**pavlova**: a dessert claimed by both Australia (some say the national dish) and New Zealand in which a soft-centered meringue is filled with a cream-and-passionfruit mixture; named for the Russian ballerina Anna Pavlova.

**pithiviers** (pee-tee-VYAY): a round tart of puff-pastry filled with almond cream (*frangipane*).

**plated**: several different items arranged on a plate, as in "Plated Dessert."

**pound cake**: a loaf cake made with equal parts flour, sugar, butter, and eggs.

**praline**: a crunchy, candy-like preparation made of crushed almonds and/or hazelnuts and caramelized sugar, used as a garnish or filling in desserts.

**profiterole**: a cream-puff dessert filled with cream or ice cream and often served with hot chocolate sauce.

**religieuse** (ruh-lee-JYUZ): usually a small pastry made of chocolate éclairs arranged in a pyramid, piped with mocha buttercream, whose color is said to resemble the homespun habit worn by French nuns, hence the name.

**sablé** (SA-blay): a French butter and sugar cookie with a "sandy" texture.

**sacher torte**: rich chocolate Viennese layer cake filled with apricot jam and coated with chocolate glaze, always served with whipped cream; named for the famed Sacher Hotel in Vienna, where it was created in the mid-nineteenth century.

**sabayon**: see Zabaglione.

**saint-honoré**: a French gateau, named for the patron saint of bakers and pastry cooks, made with a shortcrust base, a caramel-glazed puff pastry on top, and a garnish of cream puffs arranged in a ring to form a sort of crown. The whole thing is filled with cream.

**savoiardi**: Italian-style ladyfingers, the sponge-cake-like cookies often used to make tiramisú.

**semifreddo**: a "half-frozen" mousse-like mixture not made in an ice cream maker but in a mold in the freezer; semi-freddi have an airy texture as whipped cream or meringue.

**sfogliatelle** (sfol-ya-TEL-eh): a Neapolitan flaky pastry in the shape of a clamshell filled with a ricotta/semolina mixture.

**soufflé**: a light dessert containing cream, sugar, and egg yolks into which beaten whites are folded causing the mixture to puff up during baking.

**streusel**: the crumbly topping, comprised of flour, sugar and butter, and sometimes spices and nuts, sprinkled on cakes and pastries.

**strudel**: a pastry made of sheets of very thin dough filled usually with fruit (apple is most popular) or sweetened cheese and rolled, baked and served cut in slices; a specialty of Austria and Germany. (The word means "eddy" or "whirlpool" in German.)

**struffoli**: Italian Christmas pastry comprised of tiny, fried balls of dough that are arranged in a wreath shape and coated with honey or caramel.

**tarte tatin**: an apple tart in which the apples are cooked "upside down" with the fruit at the bottom of the pan in butter and sugar and the pastry on top; served inverted so the caramelized apples are on top; named after the Tatin sisters from the Loire region of France; also made with pears; first served at Maxim's in Paris.

**tiramisú**: a rich coffee-flavored dessert from Treviso, near Venice, consisting of ladyfingers (or sponge cake) soaked with espresso syrup and brandy, layered with a mascarpone-whipped cream mixture and topped with whipped cream and cocoa powder or shaved chocolate; there are hundreds of variations.

**torta**: Italian word for "cake."

**tuile** (tweel): a thin, delicate cookie that is shaped while still hot.

**vacherin** (vash-RAN): a dessert made of rings of meringue piped on top of each other to form a shell, which is then filled with ice cream or whipped cream and sometimes garnished with candied fruit; named for a round white cheese of the same name, which it resembles.

**viennoiserie**: at a French bakery, non-bread items such as croissants, brioche, and the like.

**zabaglione**; **zabaione** (zag-bal-YOH-neh): a foamy Italian dessert in which egg yolks, sweet wine, and sugar are whisked together over low heat to make a light custard; in French, *sabayon*.

**zuppa inglese** (zoopa-een-GLAZE-a): literally "English soup"; an Italian dessert, similar to English trifle, made from rum-moistened sponge cake layered with pastry cream, often decorated with chocolate shavings and candied fruit.

# favorite neighborhood bakeries and cafes

## CHELSEA

### La Bergamote
*169 Ninth Avenue at 20th Street*
PHONE: 212-627-9010
French pastries, with an emphasis on mousse cakes, in an appealing cafe setting.

### Taylor's
*228 West 18th Street bet. Seventh and Eighth Avenues*
PHONE: 212-378-2895
A mini bakery/cafe chain with hefty cookies, squares (we like the crumble-topped key lime), brownies at least 3 ways, chocolate cakes, and more.
OTHER LOCATIONS: 156 Chambers St. bet. Greenwich St. and West Broadway, 212-378-3401; 352 Hudson St. bet. Charles and West 10th Sts., 212-378-2890; 175 Second Ave. bet. 11th and 12th Sts., 212-378-2892.

## EAST VILLAGE

### Cremcaffe
*65 Second Avenue bet. 3rd and 4th Streets*
PHONE: 212-674-5255
Everyone says it: go for the chocolate crepes.

## Moishe's Kosher Bake Shop

*115 Second Avenue bet. 6th and 7th Streets*

PHONE: 212-505-8555

*504 Grand Street bet. Columbia and Willets Streets*

PHONE: 212-673-5832

Hamantaschen, rugelach, strudel, and other kosher sweets that East Village regulars swear by.

## Tarallucci e Vino

*163 First Avenue at 10th Street*

PHONE: 212-388-1190

A cozy corner cafe serving excellent panini, and a large selection of pastries and dolci, including tarallucci, the Abruzzese semolina cookies made for dunking in vino.

### FINANCIAL DISTRICT

## Cookie Island

*189 Broadway bet. Cortlandt and Dey Streets*

PHONE: 888-266-5434

A fun all-the-cookies-you-can-eat destination for kids.

### GRAMERCY

## Musette

*228 Third Avenue at 19th Street*

PHONE: 212-477-3777

Takeout French pastries and tarts, crème brûlée, carrot cake, and adorable butter animal cookies.

## Friend of a Farmer

*77 Irving Place*

PHONE: 212-477-2188

Rustic Americana-style brunch place with a sidewalk cafe

and seasonal pies worth the wait.

## GREENWICH VILLAGE

### Caffe Raffaella
*134 Seventh Avenue South bet. Charles and 10th Streets*
PHONE: 212-929-7247
So Greenwich Village, with its jumble of furniture and pastry-packed display case and the aroma of espresso in the air.

### Dean & DeLuca
*75 University Place at 10th Street*
PHONE: 212-473-1908
Not the SoHo gourmet madhouse, but a peaceful sit-down cafe in which to enjoy the good-quality pastries for which D&D is known, although without some of downtown's high-end specialties.

### Jon Vie Pastries & Café
*492 Sixth Avenue bet. 12th and 13th Streets*
PHONE: 212-242-4440
Everyone loves their danish, but they also make a mean black-and-white cookie, and the carrot cake is fine.

### Magnolia Bakery
*401 Bleecker Street at 11th Street*
PHONE: 212-462-2572
The limos still wait curbside for their cupcake-mad, banana-pudding craving, layer-cake loving clients to emerge from this tiny bakery that is approaching landmark-status.

### Marquet Patisserie
*15 East 12th Street bet. Fifth Avenue and University Place*
PHONE: 212-229-9313

Charming patisserie/cafe whose specialty is the Fraisier, the prettiest, green-iced strawberry cake in town.

OTHER LOCATIONS: 221 Court St., Cobble Hill, Brooklyn, 718-852-9267; 680 Fulton St., bet. S. Elliott Pl. and S. Portland Ave., Fort Greene, Brooklyn, 718-596-2018

## Patisserie Claude

*187 West 4th bet. Sixth and Seventh Avenues*

PHONE: 212-255-5911

Grumpy Claude might hang up on you, but he makes excellent, inexpensive tarts and cakes.

### LOWER EAST SIDE AND SOHO

## The Doughnut Plant

*379 Grand Street bet. Essex and Norfolk Streets*

PHONE: 212-505-3700

Mark Isreal's popular, oversized doughnuts have a cult following (also available at Dean & DeLuca).

## Café Lebowitz

*14 Spring Street cor. of Elizabeth Street*

PHONE: 212-219-2399

One of the best cheesecakes in town and world-class apple strudel, too—served in charmingly faux Old Viennese style.

### MIDTOWN

## Buttercup Bake Shop

*973 Second Avenue bet. 51st and 52nd Streets*

PHONE: 212-350-4144

Cupcakes and more courtesy of an alumna of Magnolia Bakery.

## Columbus Bakery

*957 First Avenue bet. 52nd and 53rd Streets*
PHONE: 212-421-0334
*474 Columbus Avenue bet. 82nd and 83rd Streets*
PHONE: 212-724-6880
Cafeteria-style bakery cafe for meals and homey pastries.

## Cupcake Cafe

*522 Ninth Avenue at 39th Street*
PHONE: 212-465-1530
Funky little takeout bakery with a surprise: amazingly
decorated cakes for all occasions.

### TRIBECA

## Duane Park Patisserie

*179 Duane Street bet. Greenwich and Harrison Streets*
PHONE: 212-274-8447
An out-of-the-way little gem with beautifully decorated and
delicious butter cookies, outstanding cakes, an awesome
lemon tart, a perfect little brownie and special-order cakes
all courtesy of Madeline Lanciani.

### UPPER EAST SIDE

## Glaser's Bake Shop

*1670 First Avenue bet. 87th and 88th Streets*
PHONE: 212-289-2562
Old-fashioned down-home baked goods since 1902.

## La Maison du Chocolat

*1018 Madison Avenue bet. 81st and 82nd Streets*

PHONE: 212-744-7117

*30 Rockefeller Center at 49th Street*

PHONE: 212-265-9404

Very fine French chocolates and outstanding ganache-based
pastries, optimally enjoyed in the uptown location's cocoa-
colored tearoom.

## Melange Food Fair

*1277 First Avenue bet. 68th and 69th Streets*

PHONE: 212-535-7773

Honey-drenched Middle Eastern pastries made by the
Egyptian-born El-Naggar brothers.

## Two Little Red Hens

*1652 Second Avenue bet. 85th and 86th Streets*

PHONE: 212-452-0476

*1112 Eighth Avenue bet. 11th and 12th Streets, Brooklyn*

PHONE: 718-499-8108

Worth the trip for pudding-filled, fudge-topped Brooklyn
Blackout cupcakes and hazelnut velvet cake.

## William Greenberg Jr. Desserts

*1000 Madison Avenue bet. 82nd and 83rd Streets*

PHONE: 212-744-0304

Venerable old-time chocolate cake source.

## Yura & Company

*1624/1659 Third Avenue at 93rd Street*

*1292 Madison Avenue at 92nd Street*

PHONE: 212-860-8060

At Third Avenue, a gleaming white, loft-style open-kitchen,
popular with after-schoolers and their moms for cupcakes,

cookies, tea cakes and more; at Madison Avenue, sit-down cafe dining with the same good pastries.

## UPPER WEST SIDE

### Levain Bakery

*167 West 74th Street bet. Columbus and Amsterdam Avenues*
PHONE: 212-874-6080
The biggest dang cookies in town—weigh 'em. Six ounces a piece, and the chocolate chip is a three-mealer.

### Margot Patisserie

*2109 Broadway at 74th Street*
PHONE: 212-721-0076
*1212 Lexington Avenue bet. 83rd and 84th Streets*
PHONE: 212-772-6064
In the French style, light and lovely pastries and cookies.

### Silver Moon Bakery

*2740 Broadway at 105th Street*
PHONE: 212-866-4717
Owner Judith Norell, formerly a harpsichordist, sometimes hosts musical events at this place popular with Columbia students known for great artisanal bread, pastries, and cookies.

### Zabar's

*2245 Broadway bet. 80th and 81st Streets*
PHONE: 212-787-2000
Home-baked strudels—apple, apricot, cherry cheese, choco-late cheese, pineapple cheese—at only $4.99 are reason enough to make a special trip to the great market.

# index

new york's 50+ best places to enjoy dessert

# index
## by neighborhood

## Upper West Side

## Brooklyn